THIS GOOD BOOK

BOOK

IAIN HOOD

RENARD PRESS

RENARD PRESS LTD

Kemp House
152–160 City Road
London EC1V 2NX
United Kingdom
info@renardpress.com
020 8050 2928

www.renardpress.com

This Good Book first published by Renard Press Ltd in 2021

Thanks are given to Mogwai for permission to quote their lyrics. Extracts on p. 17 (from 'A Cheery Wave from Stranded Youngsters'), p. 19 (from 'Yes! I am a Long Way from Home'), pp. 88–89 (from 'Tracy'), p. 99 (from 'Now You're Taken') and p. 135 (from 'Take Me Somewhere Nice') © Mogwai, All Rights Reserved

Cover design by Will Dady

Printed in the UK by CPI Group (UK) Ltd, Croydon CR0 4YY

Paperback ISBN: 978-1-913724-19-1
e-book ISBN: 978-1-913724-56-6

9 8 7 6 5 4 3 2 1

CONTENTS

THIS GOOD

BOOK

The heresies we should fear are those which can
be confused with orthodoxy.

JORGE LUIS BORGES

(trans. James E. Irby)

'The Theologians'

I

There was only one man I knew who was exactly six feet tall, and I met him in Glasgow in 1988, in the February. He caught my eye because of the colour of his flesh in the light coming through the darkened hallway at a party in a flat on Hyndland Road. Straight away I said to Stephen, 'Who is he?'

Looking over, Stephen said, 'Oh, that's Douglas.' Then he turned to me and said, 'Susan Alison MacLeod! Look at the look on you!'

And I said, 'He's the one. Look at the tone of his flesh. Like a Lucian Freud.'

And Stephen said, '"Flesh"? Do you mean skin, Susan Alison?'

And I said, 'I know what I mean and Freud paints flesh.'

Douglas stretched to open the double doors into the kitchen and his white cable-knit rode up to reveal his centre at his belly button. His flesh was yellow ochre and burnt sienna and raw umber and there was a halo of pale blue-white fluorescent light around his head and shoulders. The light around him in the darkness of the hallway formed a circle, and the door frame formed a square. He moved his legs into an isosceles of reflected light from the fake white and blue diamond tile linoleum floor. Eight heads high. The perfection of the proportion of him. The luminousness of him. His hair and moustache and beard were like a young Peter Green, if you know who Peter Green is.

And Stephen said, 'You're thinking of meat, perhaps?'

And I said, 'I'm thinking of my Crucifixion.'

And Stephen said, 'Anyway, you know him, Susan Alison. Douglas MacDougal's all over the Art School like a rash.'

And I said, 'I don't know him from Adam.'

And Stephen said, 'You have to.'

And I said, 'I've never seen him before in my puff. Cross my heart and hope to die.'

Douglas was talking to some fresher or other, looming over her.

And Stephen said, 'Do you want me to introduce you, Suse?'

And I said, 'No, not just yet. I just want to stand here watching him. But I want you to, after.'

Douglas was stretching his arms above his head and stifling a yawn, and then yawning with an unlit smoke lolling at the side of his mouth.

And Stephen said, 'Are you in love or something? He's just a man. Just flesh and blood like you and me and all the rest of us in here.'

And I said, 'You know it's bigger than that. He's the one for my Crucifixion. The end.'

Sometimes I wonder, if I had known that it was going to take me fourteen years to paint this painting of the Crucifixion with Douglas as Jesus, and what it would take for me to paint this painting, would I have been as happy as I was then?

Stephen started bouncing around and said, 'Amen. *In nomine Patris et Filii et Spiritus Sancti.*'

If it sounds like we were a bit drunk, that's because that was the way it was.

Was there always something tragic about Douglas, like he was going to die young and leave a beautiful corpse? Like in the summer, the day he came back from Glastonbury smelling of man and bonfire and lightly fried plantain and good sweat and three-day-worn clothes and his skin golden burnt and his hair just-so sun-bleached? He could not be a better Christ on the cross. God-made man, all man. The more I looked at the sky-baby-blue of his eyes. Like Zeffirelli's Jesus of Nazareth and the shallow beauty of Robert Powell's eyes that apparently got him the part. I didn't want to go for a brutal rendering. Matthias Grünewald's lip-smacking relish at twisting the emaciated body of Christ as he tortures the paint and makes Christ bleed near-solid gobbets of blood. Or Nikolai Ge's hideously terrifying and terrified Christ screaming at the top of his lungs to the sky and a God who cannot be there as his bedraggled rags soak with blood-red paint. A beautiful, western-idealised, perfect Jesus was the point and the reason and the joke, and though perhaps always tragic Douglas did like to laugh, and he liked the joke. It was part of the reason he wanted to do it. But that was later.

When Stephen introduced us, Douglas was so drunk he was close to incoherent. He said to us, 'Ask me what kinda car I want.'

And Stephen said, 'What kind of car do you want?'

And Douglas said, 'A Jaguar. Now ask me what kinda guitar I like.'

And I said, 'OK. What kind of guitar do you like?'

And he said, 'A Jaguar. See what I'm saying? A *Fender* Jaguar. Now ask me what my favourite animal is.'

And I said, 'Is it a jaguar?'

And Douglas goes, 'What? No. It's a lion, isn't it? A lion is the king of the jungle. A jaguar? That's like… that's like the Duke of Windsor or the Earl of Gloucester in comparison to the King. Heh, I was staying in Notting Hill last year, and all the pubs were like The Earl of Gloucester and the Duke of… they don't name their pubs down there, they give them a title.'

He was so drunk.

When I asked him if he'd model for me for a Crucifixion, he said he wanted to do it because of the paintings of Francis Bacon and I said, 'Oh, you like the paintings of Francis Bacon?'

And he said, 'Crucifixion? Three Studies for a Crucifixion? *Three Studies for Figures at the Base of a Crucifixion?*'

And I said, 'You like them?'

And he said, 'No! Ever since I saw them I've been trying to obliterate them from my mind, and you painting me as Christ on the cross is about the best way I can think of, eh, of annihilating those images. Annihilating them! To extirpate them from my memory.' He liked words. Concepts. Ideas. Words. And he said, 'You kill me, so you do.'

By the end of the night he was telling me that, with him in tow, I was going to create something authentic and genuine and a masterpiece and something that was *good*. And, after Stephen had disappeared somewhere, Douglas kept rocking back and forth and circling me, never still, every so often suddenly balancing himself with his outstretched arms as though the floor was tilting, as though we were on a ship far out at sea, or like he was a cat landing after being shoved off of somewhere high up.

We weren't talking, just looking around ourselves, when I heard it – just beyond hearing or something like it could be felt, even if not heard, a sound like sad, longing music. It was like I could make it be heard if I just let myself sing it, so I started singing to him this strange song about old songs and sad songs and being reminded of friends and about fairgrounds and road signs.

And Douglas said, 'What's that you're singing?'

And I said, 'I don't know. Mibby a song I heard somewhere. It's playing in my ears. Or… I think it might be a song that hasn't been written yet.'

And he said, 'You're writing this song?'

And I said, 'I… Yes. No. I mean… I don't know.' My head was swirling.

Of course, because Stephen had disappeared, it was muggins here that had to help Douglas get home. It was like trying to get a six-foot-high stack of cheese-and-ham toasties and art textbooks piled up on a skateboard home.

When we got to the mouth of his close I sort of stopped holding him up and said, 'In you go.'

He swayed for a wee while. Then he looked round at me, kind of glaikit looking, drunk glaikit, and I was wondering whether this actually was the right close, but I didn't see I had many options to find out otherwise. He stumbled forward and off he went when I pointed and repeated, 'In.'

In them days in the 80s every artist in Glasgow was buying or renting or squatting in Tollcross and environs to be near the Transmission Gallery and yes, I had been to Transmission in the year it opened and I had been inspired to go to the Art School because of what I had heard of the artists who started Transmission. But for my sins the year I graduated I found a space, a place to live with a studio attached, out along Argyle Street towards the Kelvingrove and yes, OK, near the Park Bar, where island people and teuchters drank when in Glasgow, though I never went in there because teuchters were what I sought to fly away from.

It was a garden flat that in the back yard had a huge high-walled, high-windowed transparent flat-roofed space that had housed a bakery. Have you ever had dreams where suddenly you find some incredible space in your home that you never realised before was there? A terraced penthouse accessed by way of your loft skylight or a basement that lies below your living-room floorboards? I've had those dreams and I assume they're common enough. Well, my bakery space was like that. It was like a heaven-sent dream space, unbelievably useful to an artist.

As for that part of Glasgow, I think perhaps you would call it Sandyford. I hear it's rebranded as Finnieston these days – for why, I don't know. A river crossing – the sandy ford of yore, I doubt – remained prominent down by the Clyde, and the local post office was called Sandyford Post Office. It was a quiet area then, to the point of forsaken. The first spring evening when he arrived at 7:25, the sun was going down, and as we walked into the space the sky was orange and red and purple and you could see all these colours through the transparent plastic corrugated roof of the bakery space and Douglas said to me, 'This place is perfect.'

And I said, 'Isn't it paradise?'

And he said, 'Halfway to Paradise, anyway.'

He was talking about football. Paradise is what they call Celtic's ground.

And then he said, 'The way the light comes down. Amazing. I can see why you're working on a Crucifixion.'

And I said, 'Yes. Though I was thinking about it before I came here. It just felt like a miracle to find this place.'

And he said, 'Perfect. Sure.' He looked at the piles of wood and other mess around the walls and on the floors and said, 'You can do something monumental here. Something like Howson.'

And I said, 'I was thinking more Bellany. *Allegory*.'

And he said, 'Allegory?'

And I said, 'You don't know it? Triptych. Scene of crucifixion. Of fish.'

And he was like, 'Eh?'

And I said, 'Hung, disembowelled fish.'

And he said, 'You mean gutted.'

And I said, 'No, they look more disembowelled. I know what I mean.'

And he said, 'Of course you do, Susan Alison. Have you ever been fishing?'

And I was like, 'No, have you?'

And he said, 'What? You're kidding, right? Fishing? Me? That'll be right.'

Right. So. You'll know Douglas's art. He filled plastic bags with his own urine. I know what you're thinking. 'So… modern.'

Much later I remember saying to him, 'You're what gives modern art a bad name.'

And he was like, 'Me, is it? As long as I'm giving it a name.'

And I said, 'Did you ever hear that thing about the Ancient Egyptians or the Aztecs or the Huns?'

And he said, 'The Huns?'

And I said, 'Yes. You know, Attila and the Huns. Attila the Hun and the other…'

And he was like, 'Huns?'

And I said, 'Yes.'

And he said, 'Oh, I know all about the Huns.'

That was about football in Glasgow, too.

And I said, 'Yes, well, did you know that we call them these things like the Mayans and the Ancient Greeks but their names for themselves all translate from their languages as "the moderns"? Did you know that?'

And he was like, 'Where do you get this stuff?'

And I said, 'Books. Good books. Like this good book.' I held one up and showed him, a 1981 Oxford World's

Classics copy of *The Private Memoirs and Confessions of a Justified Sinner* – the one with the Henry Fuseli cover.

And he said, 'Aye. TV. So what about the Moderns? Nineteen-twenties Paris Moderns?'

And I said, 'I suppose they called themselves "the moderns". And people now call them Modernists. In the islands, they say "modren" for "modern". For why, I've no idea.'

And he said, 'Do you think it's like the way that "hundreds" becomes "hunners"?'

And I said, 'Yes. Mibby. Though that's the other way up from modern and modren. The other way round.'

And he said, 'Do you know about Piero Manzoni?'

And I said, 'Who?'

And he said, 'Artist. Italian. Nineteen fifties or there-abouts. Sold his own shite in tins.'

And I said, 'And people bought it?'

And he was like, 'Absolutely.'

And I said, 'A major influence on you?'

And he was like, 'Oh yes.'

And I said, 'Nice oeuvre.'

And he said, 'Nice. It's what all artists are doing. Selling their shite. They say it. This is my shite. I want to sell my shite.'

And I said, 'I get you now. You're a cynic.'

And he said, 'You're a funny girl.'

And I was like, 'Girl?'

And he said, 'Right. Aye. Right. Sorry.'

And I said, 'You know there was one time I was at school, down by the huts and...' But then, no, I couldn't tell him *that* story. He didn't seem to have heard me, anyway.

And he said, 'Anyway. Don't put me off my... Manzoni, he was a Modernist.'

And I said, 'Yes? Futurist, mibby.'

And Douglas said, 'Aye! Exactly. He sold his own shite. Naw?'

A while later Douglas said, 'Naw. A gallery of modern Scottish art? In Glasgow? I'm not sure that's happening any time soon. But you never know.'

And I said, 'Why not?'

And he said, 'A celebration of contemporary... of modern art? In Glasgow? All very well for fancy-schmancy Edinburgh, but Glasgow? I'm not sure you know where you live.'

We were standing in the Glasgow Art Gallery in Kelvingrove. He was wrong, by the way. I was right, by the way. A gallery of modern art did open in Glasgow seven years after this conversation. But back then I'm not sure even he thought this was a good idea. Mibby just wanted to stick with his Transmission pals. Yes. I see now. Mibby that was it.

Douglas said, 'All right. How many times have you stood here before this one?'

And I said, 'Hundreds?' I shrugged and then I said, 'Thousands? Hundreds, anyway.'

And he said, 'And what draws you back?'

And pointing as though they were there I said, 'The nails. The blood. The crown of thorns.'

And Douglas looked up and after a minute said, 'But the painting doesn't depict any of those things.'

And I said, 'I know. Their absence was the first thing I noticed. Dalí said the image came to him in a dream and he said he had to paint it without these things because they would undermine the perfection of the image of Christ.'

And Douglas was like, 'And why is it *Christ of St John of the Cross?*'

And I said, 'John of the Cross. Juan de la Cruz. A Spanish mystic. He sketched a Crucifixion with Christ in the same posture. Sagging from the cross. Dalí wanted a triangular arrangement with a circle formed by the head. The trinity. The whole. The four elements. It's a masonic symbol.'

And he said, 'Masonic? Lodge people? Orangemen?'

And I said, 'No, that's a misnomer. Orange Lodge is a masonic thing...'

And he was like, 'Moronic?'

And I said, 'Yes, good one. But the Freemasons weren't Orangemen. In Italy, the masons were Catholics. And, anyway, then the Pope said, "No secret societies," like he isn't in one, and the Church went anti-Freemason. But then, I think Freemasons were just about anti everything that wasn't Freemasonry... so... there you go. A-one two three four five six seven eight, a-one two three four five six and on you go.'

He looked at me and smiled, swear to God, and he said, 'You kill me, Susan Alison, you really do.'

And looking up at Dalí's painting I said, 'Look at it. It's miraculous. See the use of the golden ratio, there, there, here and there.'

And he said, 'That's the *a* is to *b* as...'

And I said, 'Yes, *a* plus *b* is to *a* as *a* is to *b*. See it? Dalí was saying that there is a sacred geometry, a god behind nature. Or at least a god behind art.'

And he said, 'Aye? Aye, himself.'

And I said, 'You might be right.'

He stared at it for a good long while, then he said, 'It gives me a feeling.'

And I said, 'I should hope so.'

And he said, 'Aye. Something like... I'm out in space.'

And I said, 'Yes? Well, thank you, space expert.'

And he said, 'Aye.' He looked more, screwing up his eyes, and said, 'Yes.'

And I said, 'Something else?'

And he said, 'Something... something like... Yes, I am a long way from home. Aye. Yes, exclamation mark! I am a long way from home!'

And I said, 'Oh, yes, it needs that − it needs the exclamation mark, sure sure.'

And he said, 'I *am* a long way from home.'

And I said, 'I am a *long* way from home!'

And he was like, 'Here, haud on, I'm a long way from *home*!?'

And I said, 'Oh aye. Very good.'

And he said, 'What's wrong with your eyes?'

And I said, 'My eyes? How?' Except it didn't come out as 'How?' It was more like 'Howh?' 'Howwuuh?' Something like that. Like time was slowing down as I said the word, but just for me and not the rest of the world. And that's when I dropped to the floor.

And he said he was like, 'Susan Alison! Suse! What is this? What should I do?'

I wasn't writhing around or whatever... like whatever people with epilepsy are supposed to do. I've only ever seen one person with epilepsy having a seizure and he wasn't doing any of that, anyway. He just looked blank and empty like the human being inside of him was gone. And I think from the outside that's what I looked like, too. But in myself I felt all serene and good and full of... light? Light, mibby? Colour? I knew the definite shapes around me. There was a taste in my mouth mibby like metal and my mouth was filling up with the taste of mibby metal and more than anything else I could hear... like music far off and a rhythm and a line of melody, repeating once, twice... then again.

And I knew I was saying stuff. About music which can put a human being in a trance-like state. About the sneaking feeling of existing. And about music being bigger than words and wider than pictures. That Mogwai are the stars. I would not object. That if the stars had a sound it would sound like this. And that the punishment for these solemn words can be hard. And about how my blood boils like this at the sound of a noisy tape that I've heard. And that I knew one thing. On Saturday... the sky will crumble... together − or something − with a huge bang... to fit into the cave. And clapping and music gurgled. And as something like a heartbeat of guitars got noisier and noisier I remember I was thinking and wanted to say to Douglas in capitals, ''*ART SYMBOLISES THE MEANING OF OUR EXISTENCE*" − *ANDREI TARKOVSKY*.' Not shouting at him and not shouting over the noise of the guitars like the uppercase letters suggest, but just I saw it that way in my mind's eye, in upper case.

When I came to, after the final crash of cymbals and guitars and laughing or talking or something playing back to front in my ears, I was like, 'Man, sorry about that.'

He took me to the Gallery café and because I was shivering made me drink a cup of milky tea with about five or six teaspoons of sugar in it, which he said was what his mother always gave him and his sisters and brothers when they seemed sickly or overheated or whatever, this being her personal panacea for all life's ills.

And Douglas was like, 'Well, that was a bit freaky. Are you OK? Has that happened before?'

And I said, 'I'm brand new. Why?'

And he said, 'You just freaked me out is all.'

When it seemed as though I could, and he was puffed out on sympathy and questions and advice to see a doctor, I finally changed the subject and said, 'Do you know Dalí's other Crucifixion?'

And he said, 'Aye, the *Corpus Hypercube*?'

And I said, 'So you know something about traditional art as well, then? I thought that wasn't encouraged in Conceptual and Performance.'

He bowed and tipped an imaginary hat, then he said, 'Aye? Snob.'

And I said, 'Yes, I am a snob when it comes to art, as a matter of fact. Taste and distinction and judgement are everything.'

And he said, 'Aye? I'll be the judge of that. And I know one or two things. Though, have to admit, I know Dalí's moustache more than I know his art. And anyway, my art is pure taste. You can taste it. It's all in the taste.'

I forgot to mention the Tarkovsky thing.

Thing is, in the summer, in the August, I was back up on the island visiting my mithair and faither and I was telling my mithair all about him and I said to her, 'Oh, if only you could see him, Mummy.' I had no photographs. A Polaroid or a disposable or a PhotoMe booth passport photo would just not have done him justice and a good film camera was well beyond my means with me being impecunious, as my faither said. And so anyway, I said, 'If only you could see him. So beautiful and with goodness in his eyes and his flesh.'

And my mithair said, 'Flesh?'

And I said, 'Skin. So unblemished and oh, now, Mummy, he's tall. Exactly six feet tall.'

And my mithair said, 'Dear Lord, no, Susan Alison. There was only ever one man as was exactly six feet tall. Your Lord and Saviour Jesus Christ.'

And I said, 'Fine. Well he's almost exactly six feet tall and if of all men only Jesus was exactly six feet tall then that makes Douglas an even more perfect model, don't you think? What are you like?'

And she said, 'Stop that.'

And I said, 'Stop what?'

And Mummy said, 'That way you're getting of talking. Like the way they talk down in Glasgow. "What am I like?" Indeed.'

And I said, 'I'm not… All I'm trying to tell you about is Douglas.'

And Mummy said, 'Fine, but if you're going to tell me about him at least make it a story and tell me it from the start. And don't skip details.'

So I started to tell her the story, not skipping any details I thought she would want to hear. She seemed to be listening quietly, and as I got to the part about paint-ing a Crucifixion scene with Douglas as Jesus she stirred and said, 'I want you to be doing good paintings of your Saviour. Are you doing good paintings?'

Like all good Christians, she wanted good paintings of suffering and torture and death and rape and incest and child sacrifice and bestiality. Good Bible stories. Good paintings.

And my mithair said, 'Not that pornography that some people do. Or the paintings by grown-ups who paint like children or the twizzles and wizzles people or those ones that paint a red circle and say it's art. The Devil's work, I call that.'

And I said, 'Yes, I am, Mummy, I am, yes, good paint-ings.'

And my mithair said, 'You know, sometimes I think you don't know Jesus, Susan Alison. Down there in Glasgow you're not being taken in by those so and sos, are you?'

And I said, 'Yes Mummy, I am not,' not bothering a toffee that I was lying.

II

Things were taking a lot longer to get together than I had thought they would and I wasn't getting to know Douglas much better, even though this didn't bother me the way, you know, some artists need to know the insides of their sitters, but that wasn't going to be necessary for my Crucifixion. Creating art, and I mean specific art, you have to know what's going to be necessary, this being the mother of invention and all that, you know?

He was in his world with his Tollcross buddies and I was in Sandyford making preparations for painting my Crucifixion, what with buying materials and paints and nailing together canvases that were so huge I had to use huge nails to secure them. And the size of the hammer I had to buy! My God! And I'm only five foot nothing. Apart from the time I had let him come to the bakery studio to have a look around and the times we had visited galleries and stuff like that, we went on with our separate lives. I was experimenting with different backgrounds and thinking mibby about doing a Stanley Spencer by setting the Crucifixion on top of the Necropolis, but that was too obvious, or mibby doing a Billy Connolly by painting something called something like Christ Crucified upon the Tollcross, but really only because giving the painting this title appealed to me.

Not me, but all of them, Isobel and Amanda and Marion and Anna, Jenny and Rona and Mairi, Katrina and Maureen and Alison and Bernice, Katy and Frances and Maria, Sharleen and Kate and Nikki and Shonagh and all of them at one time or another seemed to be in love with Douglas.

And I suppose that's why I was supposed to be in love with him and why I had made him my model for Christ on the cross, but it wasn't that at all. In fact, I thought he was a stupit so and so. I mean, come on. Urine in bags? What was that? That was nothing. Nothing. Just some sensationalist nonsense with apparent meaning but no meaning manifest. One of my best tutor's sayings was, and I suppose still is, 'Art is meaning manifest.' Douglas would talk of bodies and fluids and this and that. That was nothing. He had nothing. The tutor, my best tutor, would have seen right through him, all right. Miss Brodie, we called her. That wasn't her name. She was actually called Jean Carmichael, but I think the 'Jean' and the way about her led to 'Miss Brodie'. Anyway. But it has to be said, he was a good model, Douglas. He mostly knew how to pull this way and that way and take up the best version of this and that position. And he would be like, 'Is this the way you want me?'

He was malleable is what I'm saying. And beautiful. So very beautiful. And Jesus needed to be beautiful, because if he's not beautiful then what is he? Jesus as God had to be the most beautiful man and the perfection of man, because if he's not that then what is he? Douglas was malleable and if he was not malleable to what I wanted him to be in my hands then what was *he*? What *was* he?

18

But, you know, all of them loved him. Lived for the parties when they could be near him and find out what he was up to and what he was drinking and what he was saying. The time he cordoned off areas with some DO NOT CROSS THIS LINE tape at that party on Byres Road. (Where the hell does one find DO NOT CROSS THIS LINE tape? Fortuitously, on the way to a party appears to be the answer.) They wanted to know what he was doing and what it meant. 'What does it *mean*?' they asked. Just watching him cordon off. Cordoning off the living room. Oh Jesus, wasn't this the best thing ever! So creative! So unusual! What a laugh! It was, actually. It was. You should have watched him do it and the look on his face. Beatific and angelic and mischievous and devilish! You could see their point. He was loveable in the act of *cordoning*. That takes talent.

Anyway, next thing is either Isobel or Jenny or Mairi or Katrina or Maureen or Katy or Frances or Shonagh would be saying to me, 'Who is he?' or, 'Is that Douglas MacDougal?' or, worst of all, 'Are you *with* Douglas?'

And I was thinking, 'I'm going to *make* this guy because *his* art is nothing and *my* art is meaning manifest and is going to make *him* famous,' and for just one second I was like, 'Drop the guy, he's not the model for Jesus for you,' but it only lasted a second and then I was like, 'Look at him. *Look* at him and his beautiful *triceps*. So beautiful. Forget dropping him. He's the one, even as bag of hammers as he is.'

Then one night I was standing with him and hadn't seen him for a few weeks and one of them, one of Alison or Katy or Frances... whoever it was, said to him, 'I heard about you last night.'

19

And he said, 'Aye?'

And Alison or Maureen or Katy or Frances or whoever said, 'Oh aye.'

And he said, 'Aye, well it's all true. Naw. Actually it's all lies.'

And Bernice or Maureen or whoever said, 'Thought so. What are you like?'

And he just said nothing and had a Goofy smile on him like an idiot. And when Maureen walked away, because it was Maureen, when I come to think about it, I said, 'What was that all about?'

And Douglas said, 'Search me.'

And I looked at him and he caught me looking and I was giving him a right dirty look.

And he said, 'Search me. Honestly. I stayed in and worked last night.'

And I said, 'Worked? You mean you had a few pishes?'

And he said, 'Worked on the concept. How it should develop. What it might mean.'

And I said, 'Of course.'

And he was like, 'Really.'

And I said, 'You should be a novelist, you make up such extravagant stories.'

And he said, 'Aye, right. Novelists are just like lazy conceptual artists who just tell their readers, "Imagine a world like this," and don't even bother their arses to paint or build this world or film it or sculpt it or do anything else to actually represent it.'

And I said, 'So there's nothing that could have been heard when she said that she heard about you last night?'

And he said, 'That's right.'

And I was like, 'Don't believe you.'

And he said, 'Oh? Aye? Believe what you want.'

Just then another of them came by, and it was either Alison or Bernice or Katy or Frances, but not Maureen, and she said, 'Heh. Douglas. Heard about you last night!'

And he waved at her. Waved. And I'm like staring up at the side of his head. He turned to me and said, 'What can I tell you? Rumours fly around about me. I've no clue why.'

They probably were making up stuff about him between themselves. Marion and Anna and Jenny and Rona and Mairi and Katrina and all of them. To be honest I had heard someone tell him they had heard about what he had been up to 'last night' once when the night before I had spent my time with him planning how I could hang him from a wall. But it was just. Well. It was just. Just… annoying. They were like planets forever falling towards him like he was the sun.

When the sun came up it was a Tuesday morning and it hit me straight in the eyes: I had forgotten to close the blind the night before. My eyes flickered open and in an intense yellow light immediately shut again and I saw the vermillion red of my blood in the skin of my eyelids. It wasn't even that early and my alarm clock had already gone off and been silenced. That's the morning I decided that summer was moving on too fast and I had to tell Douglas the way I wanted to paint him and show him an Eric Gill I had found in this good book about Gill.

And when I got to see him and told him he said, 'Did you hear the rumours about Eric? The shenanigans?'

And I said, 'I know about Eric Gill. And I know all about the shenanigans. An honest artist who became dishonest.'

And he said, 'How do you reckon that?'

And I said, 'He did a brilliant Crucifixion in nineteen ten which caused a lot of controversy, as it should have. What's the point of an uncontroversial Crucifixion? Some Stanley Spencer anodyne piece of nonsense?'

And he said, 'What did Gill do that was so admirably controversial, then?'

And I said, 'Christ naked upon the cross.'

And he said, 'And then?'

And I was like, 'Pandemonium. People went bananas, saying it was immoral. A naked Christ. Christ! In nineteen ten with Queen Victoria's eldest boy barely cold in his grave! Can you imagine?'

And Douglas said, 'Aye, but what did Gill do after that? I mean after you've done a naked Christ there's not many places you can go.'

And I said, 'That's probably why he became a backslider. He did a lot more Crucifixion scenes, but none of a naked Christ. By nineteen seventeen he was so pastel he was allowed to do the Stations of the Cross in Westminster Cathedral. What's that sound?'

And Douglas said, 'What sound?'

And I said, 'Like a piano.'

And he said, 'I don't hear nothing. So, Eric Gill. What became of him?'

And I said, 'Oh, they'll crucify him some day. When the shenanigans are known by more people than a few art tutors with salacious tastes.'

And he said, 'How do you reckon?'

And I said, 'Oh, Douglas! He was into incest and bestiality.'

And he said, 'Aye? How very biblical of him.'

And I said, 'When a true biography comes out, not the whitewash that was published, he'll be crucified and deserve everything he gets.'

And he was like, 'And his reputation will nosedive?'

And I said, 'What? No! It'll rise and keep rising!'

And he said, 'How'll that work?'

And I said, 'Art isn't religion and religion isn't art. You know? Morality isn't art and art isn't morality.'

And he was like, 'And what about religion and morality?'

And I said, 'Trickier business. Gill's poor daughter. She'll still be alive when the true biography finally comes out. Imagine. She'll be saying it all seemed perfectly normal. That's what John said.' John was one of my tutors at the Art School.

And he said, 'Is that the way you want to paint me? Naked?'

And I said, 'Mibby. We'll talk about it later.'

After that we went to the Ubiquitous Chip up in the West End where we met a bunch of Art School people, it so happened. While we were all talking together, one of Douglas's pals said, 'Christ in the last judgment in the Sistine Chapel. Michelangelo painted that one naked. It was painted over with a cloth by later artists.'

And I said, 'Is that right? Who? Which artists?'

And the pal said, 'I don't know, do I? Just an artist or artists commissioned by the Holy Roman Catholic and Apostolic Church, I suppose.'

23

After a while and as we were getting quite drunk, what with him and his pals on pints of Fürstenburg and me having had three Kir Royales, Douglas was driving me round the bend. And the way all his stupit pals had a nickname for him, Cody, and all of them kept calling him Cody, Cody, Cody this and Cody that. Them all poking at him and saying he wasn't quite black enough to be Jesus in my painting: this was about the time of Madonna's 'Like a Prayer' video, which is supposed to have a black Jesus in it, though the black actor's actually, I'm sure, playing a saint. Not that Douglas's pals were making any kind of subtle points. They were just pissing about. And then, when I tried to make a serious point by saying that I didn't know why the Vatican were getting their panties in a ruck over a black Jesus and it was just because it was Madonna and they had been sanctioning ethnically diverse representations of Jesus in their missions for years, all I got from them was, you know, they were all like, 'Oooooooh'. And then there was just a lot of sniggering and nods and winks about who I was to him and who he was to me and about how I wanted to paint him in the nude apparently because I, like all the 'girls', found him oh so absolutely irresistible. In the name of the Father and the Son and the Holy Ghostie man.

After his friends had left, I was like, 'What was *that*?' I was total death rays coming out of my thousand-foot face.

And Douglas said, 'What?'

And I said, 'You.'

And he said, 'What?'

And I said, 'You acting like a… like…'

And he said, 'How?'

And I said, 'You just acting like a… like a…'

And he said, 'Acting how?'

And I said, 'Just acting like a wee boy with your wee mates and being a stupit... a stupit...' God, I was speechless.

And he said, 'I have no idea what you're talking about.'

Well, I saw red, didn't I? Ready to pin him against the wall. And I really went for it, giving it a load of swear words and stringing it all together and like, 'You wouldn't even know what to do with a woman if you were alone with her nude, you ——' Well, I won't repeat what I called him. It's beneath me. Really. We're bigger than that. And I said, 'Those friends of yours, forget it. They're not drinking with us any more, no way.'

And he said, 'Aye, I know. Think you were popular with them?'

And I was like, 'Man, I could just wake up and go berserk.'

And he was like, 'Look, they're my friends, they aren't me.'

And I was like, 'That lets you off, does it?'

And he was like, 'Can it. Man, leave me alone.'

And I was walking to the door to the stairs down to the street and I said, 'I will.'

I will not say that the initial stages went anything but prosaically. I was hoping for the poetry of creation, and prose is all we got. Well, you have to start somewhere, and I finally started doing initial sketches the day after he got back from Glastonbury when he was still in the same clothes he had worn the whole time and with his sunburn and tan lines and smell. Sketches of his face and his hands and his feet and of the right side of his abdomen. All the bits where the most detail was required. Then he said he was knackered from three days of no sleep and stretched out on the floor cruciform and I did some drawings with pencil on paper or charcoal on parchment. And I was saying, 'Lift your arm higher. Over your head. Stretch out. Let the muscle strain. Move round the other way. Turn more towards me. Face on. No. Turn back.' And at one point I was like, 'What's that you're doing?'

And he said, 'I'm, eh, I'm thinking of the photo of Jim Morrison on the EP *Hello I Love You*. You seen that, him in that pose?'

And I said, 'No I have not, and could you forget it?'

And he said, 'I thought that was a good one. You know the lyrics. "Hello. I love you. I'm Jim Morrison. I'm dead." Well, that's the lyrics now, anyway.'

And I said to Douglas, 'It's not working.'

And he said, 'I can tell.'

And I said, 'Mibby we need you on a cross.'

But for the time being he would lie on the ground and stretch his limbs and body into a crucifixion pose, and he lay this way and that, me sitting on a stool or up and down on a ladder if I moved across to map out anything on one of the big canvases.

And he said, 'Is it OK?'

And I said, 'Mm.'

And I began again. And sketched. And sketched. And sketched until he said, 'I have to stop. It's painful. I'm sore.'

And I said, 'OK, but just for a wee while.'

And he said, 'Anything.'

So the middle of summer passed. Him on the floor, me on the stool or up and down the ladder. The light was good, falling down upon him. And I could sketch from his feet up and his head down. But it wasn't working. I was spending money on bigger and bigger and more and more sketchbooks, and each sketch was such an abortion.

And Douglas said, 'Is this working?'

And I said, 'What?'

And he said, 'Susan?'

And I said, 'Just you stay where you are, now.'

And he was like, 'I'm getting up for a breather.'

And I said, 'Can't you just stay where you are, now? Wait... I'm just about to... I've got this.'

And he said, 'I'm getting up. It's sore.'

And I said, 'Jesus. You'd be dead now if I was my mummy or I was the way my mummy was.'

My mummy was a sixties mummy and a Jesus freak first and foremost. She loved Cat Stevens and the Fleetwood Mac Peter Green era and my dad and my brothers and sisters and me but she did not love anyone more than Jesus. Every year once a year when I was growing up one of us who was old enough would travel down to Glasgow and hand out Jesus freak pamphlets with all the other Jesus freaks in George Square, though she didn't generally like the other Jesus freaks, saying they were dirty and smelly and long-hairs and that they wore sandals, or, as they called them, Jesus boots, and one of the few times I remember her slapping me firmly across the chops was when it was my turn to be down in Glasgow with her because I had said mibby Jesus had been a dirty and smelly long-hair who wore sandals. The thing I remember most about this was that she didn't take her hand off my

27

face at the time when she was angry. She did it just as we were about to get the ferry from Oban, standing on the jetty. She hadn't said much to me on the trip home till then. Then she turned to me straight on and said I should not say such things about Jesus and then slapped me clean across my cheek. She was so calm doing it. I stood there silently cradling my cheek in my palm and knew I wasn't to say anything in response. And straight afterwards and all the rest of the way home she was calm and talked quietly when she spoke to me.

I think even then, Jesus freak or no, she also liked to believe in loads of other freaky stuff like werewolves and vampires and the dead rising from the grave and alien abductions and angels looking down on us from above. All that was just part and parcel. But mostly the suffering face of Jesus looking down upon us from the cross was what she liked to believe in.

My mithair, I told Douglas, was a one-woman sixties baby boom. When I was born I was number twelve and the last born, and my faither nodded and said to my mithair, 'An even dozen.' The only thing not Victorian about the whole deal was six or seven or eight of us were not dead before the time we were ten. Well, one died, but I won't go into that now. So there were eleven of us, with me the last. The youngest. The wee girl. The baby. Baby me. Although there were still twelve of us if you count the Baby Jesus, who was, after all, my mithair's favourite baby of all.

With my mithair it was a good thing to love God and it was a good thing to fear Satan. But then, it seemed it was also a good thing to fear God too. I used to sit sometimes for hours just thinking about loving God and fearing Satan. Hours. That's what I had been thinking when Douglas got restless and started on about how he couldn't hold position for as long as I wanted him to. He was on the floor arching his back with arms outspread.

And he said, 'What is it you are looking for, anyway?'

He was getting uncomfortable with me staring, I guess, but then, if that's going to bother you then don't sit for an artist is what I say.

And so anyway, finally he said, 'What is this? You're no painting. You're just sitting there staring. Are you going tae paint or what?'

I didn't react and I think he was getting all, 'I'm leaving if this is the deal.'

And when I finally snapped to and heard him, he was almost shouting, 'Susan Alison! Susan Alison!'

And I said, 'I'm looking for God in him. In you, I mean. I'm looking for God in you.'

And he said, 'You trying to get transcendental or something?'

And I said, 'I'm trying to be right here.'

And he said, 'Well you don't seem right here. No the now.'

And I said, 'Sorry. What were you saying?'

And he said, 'I was telling you about my work with urine.'

And I said, 'Jesus. What was it I asked you?'

And he said, 'You asked about my work and I'm telling you.'

And I said, 'You work with *urine*?'

And he said, 'Aye.'

And I said, 'How do you mean?'

And he said, 'I urinate in bags and then I seal them up. The bags are exhibited in different ways in different settings. Depends on the setting. I'm also thinking of doing some performance pieces where the bags are empty to begin with—'

And I said, 'And you pee into them as a performance?'

And he said, 'Aye! And don't say "piss artist" because everybody says that.'

And I said, 'And this is your art?'

And he's like, 'Sure. How? To be honest I'm surprised you don't know more about it. I mean, I'm getting press and that.'

And I was like, 'I bet.'

And he said, 'Aye! Good press. Got a really good review for my last piece in the Transmission. *FOURTEEN DAYS*. The reviewer said it was elemental. That my art spoke of the deep functions of the body. Elemental. I liked that. Elemental.'

III

The end of the summer was fast approaching and there-
fore it was the end of the initial time period I thought it
would take me to *finish* the Crucifixion, so there was only
one thing for it and that was to *start* painting. Honest to
God, I'm not kidding, I could have gone on sketching him
till kingdom come, but nothing was coming from that. So
I started painting and he was on the floor, limbs stretched
out, and we didn't talk much except I'd say something
like, 'Stretch your left arm more, make a fist, twist that
arm this way,' except with loads of minutes or even an
hour passing between each comment.

I thought I just needed to do some fast paintings.
Though, obviously, the word 'fast' is a relative term when
you are talking the size of canvas I was intent on working
on and the sheer amount of paint you have to get on
it, the sheer weight. Even just priming the monster took
ages, up and down ladders, moving from one side to the
other on a platform. Then I would sketch out the figurative elements using charcoals, then start with thinned-out
oils in natural colours before moving on to the actual
application of actual paint. All through my degree and

into the start of my working life I had been using oils
and it had all been manageable working at the scale I
had so far, which was mainly a couple of feet high by
a couple of feet wide, and I wanted to stick with my
preferred medium. It was just going to be a whole lot
of bloody hard work.

Then, one Sunday session with me painting on one
of the big canvases I turned and saw that his eyes were
closed and his muscles had relaxed, though he was still
softly maintaining the cruciform position. I walked over
to look down at him and he was snoring lightly. He'd
been on the randan with his Transmission pals and was
done in. So I moved over to a stool to just kind of watch
him sleep. Sleeping like a baby. A big, drunk baby. He
was probably still drunk from the night before. And
then out of the blue and seemingly from the depth of
his sleep he was like, 'You've skipped a step.'

And I said, 'Is that right?'

And still snoring between words he said, 'Studies.
Studies for a Crucifixion.'

Well, he was right, wasn't he? I couldn't just move
from sketches, no matter how big these were, on to
big canvases. So for a few weeks I put together some
wee canvases, wee-er even than the couple of feet ones
I used to work on. Working on an easel and using a
maulstick too, totally trad, with Douglas pulling this
way and that so that I could paint a study of an arm,
a neck, a side of his abdomen. In the end there were
about sixty, mibby more, of these wee bits of Douglas,
like I'd chopped him up and scattered his parts all over
the studio.

Tell a lie. It was a Monday session. We never worked on a Sunday together. Don't know why I remembered it that way there. He'd been out on the ran on the Sunday.

I was using a limited palette then. White and black with mibby some highlights in blue and yellow and then mibby just two or three other colours. So, after I got back to painting on the big canvases and a few of these paintings got going I became a bit obsessed with yellow and after a break of a few days and a visit to the art supplies shop I kept the white and black and blue, but highlights were in Lemon Yellow Hue and Winsor Lemon and Cadmium Lemon, Bismuth Yellow and Transparent Yellow and Winsor Yellow. Then, after a rushed visit back to the art suppliers there was an explosion of all them plus Chrome Yellow Hue and Cadmium Yellow Pale and Indian Yellow Deep and Indian Yellow. Then Cadmium Yellow and Winsor Yellow Deep and Cadmium Yellow Deep. And then I realised it was the blue that was really the issue. So, more shopping for Indanthrene Blue and Cobalt Blue Deep and French Ultramarine and Ultramarine (Green Shade) and Winsor Blue (Red Shade) and Winsor Blue (Green Shade) and Cerulean Blue and the deep, deep blue of Cobalt Blue and Manganese Blue Hue and even Phthalo Turquoise and Cobalt Turquoise and Cobalt Turquoise Light.

And so anyway, it got to the stage that all he was really saying, because talking would just cause me to lose concentration, was things like, 'It's sore. I'll have to move a bit. Can we stop for a bit?' except with loads of time between statements. And I mean loads of time. I mean, loads and loads of time. It was actually Douglas that spotted that oils just weren't going to cut it. I mean, if you weighed out the actual weight of the paint I was humphing up on to the canvas, I mean, I don't know, but I bet it was more than the weight of me for each session we did.

We were taking a breather and he went, 'Suse, we're going to be here till we're both dead at this rate.'

And I was like, 'I know, but what can I do about it?'

And he said, 'How about bigger brushes? Like, a clennie man's street-sweeper brushes. Know what I mean? Just get the paint up there without all the up and down.'

And I said, 'You can't do oils like that.'

And he was like, 'Well, change from oils. Jeez-oh. There's not enough time in eternity to get this down.'

And I was like, 'What are you thinking? Gouache?'

And he said, 'Aye. Gouache. Acrylics. Whatever it takes. I'll even prime the canvas for you, just to do something else for a wee while.'

In the end up I chose acrylic gouache, a compromise deal. The idea was to use thinned-down paint, then move to heavier and heavier body paint as I built up the canvas and filled it with the colour I wanted. And this worked. Almost straight off I could see how the colour field and depth was going to work. And we weren't both going to be dead by the time I had a worked painting. But it still took ages, looking at him, walking up to the canvas, up the ladders or on to the platform, adding the paint which I had in bigger and bigger pots. Getting down and moving back over to look at him, look at the canvas, then back to him, then back to the monster. When he asked to stop for a second time within one session I flicked my wrist and the paint went *wheee* and I said, 'Just give me a *minute*.'

And he went, 'It's sore,' and his stomach muscles flexed like he was about to get up and my brush flicked and the paint went flying.

And I said, 'Stay where you are! For Christ's sake!'

And then, I don't know, but frustration got the better of me and the paint was flying all over and total Jackson Apollockalypse with a frenzy of dripping and throwing and flying paint was all over the shop. I was in a frenzy and Douglas was on the ground, first trying to turn this way and that so as the paint didn't get just everywhere, but eventually he gave up and was just lying there and taking it and he was like, 'OK, Suse, OK,' when the paint wasn't flying at his mouth, and he was saying, 'I get it, I get it. Get it out.' I take it he meant my frustration, but he could have been talking about the paint that was still in the tubs that I was grabbing for to chuck at him.

Anyway, I walked over to his jacket that was thrown over a chair and got his smokes out of his pocket and lit one to be like Pollock and held it in my mouth the way Pollock did and as I stood over him dripping and chucking paint I smoked and coughed and let the ash fall on him a couple of times. And the smoke rising from the smokes was blue and I kept dripping more blues on him until he said, 'I am not Batman.'

And I said, 'Eh? What?'

And he said, 'Batman. People think he's got a suit that's black but in the original comics he's always in blue.'

And I said, 'Batman. Blue?'

And he was like, 'Well. Aye. Haw. You're getting it in my mouth again, for Christ's sake.'

35

After this was kind of when we decided we mibby needed to get him on a cross and up off the ground at least, or fix up something so that he could lie against a cross. So as, at least if the kind of thing that had just happened happened again and I lost it, the paint would run off him and not get in his mouth, because paint is kind of disgusting to swallow. Know what I'm saying? A cross. An actual cross had to be the answer. I don't think I was wrong here.

Don't get me wrong here. I was doing loads of painting that was going well and I'd got a gallery in London interested in my work. After Wiszniewski and Campbell and Conroy and that lot, if you had talent then getting gallery representation could be pretty easy to come by – if, as I say, you had talent. So loads of my work was going well. But it was when I was able to get together with Douglas and start working on the Crucifixion again that everything just seemed to, I'm not sure, just not work. I just couldn't get the way I wanted to do it, so I hadn't completed a single canvas yet without painting it over with something I *could* do when Douglas wasn't around. So, nothing to show for it. Nothing to show for any of it.

Mibby it was that experience of frustration and watching his body being covered in paint that gave me my next idea, that I had to paint *him* first, and I said to Douglas, 'Is it OK if I paint you?'

And he said, 'I thought that's what you had been doing.'

And I said, 'No. I mean there's something about the light in here. It's too much. Your flesh... it's too... I don't know. I can't paint it as it is. What I'm saying is I paint you blue, some shade, first, then mibby I can paint you into the canvas. What do you think?'

And he shrugged and said, 'It's your painting.'

And I said, 'Are you going to let me paint you blue?'

And he said, 'Aye, sure, I'll experiment anything. Paint me blue, see how it goes, eh? Blues hour, man.'

So he let me paint his flesh blue. I used a liquid latex and acrylic mix Indanthrene Blue, though I realised almost straight away that it wasn't blue enough, and over the time it took to cover him I was adding wee bits of Prussian blue pigment I had left over from some woodblock prints I had been experimenting with. And I was talking to him about International Klein Blue, the bluest blue, and ultramarine, and Picasso's Blue Period, and more about Klein's *Leap into the Void*, and *the* blues and Miles Davis's *Kinda Blue* and 'Don't It Make My Brown Eyes Blue?' and about my favourite album, Joni Mitchell's *Blue*, and what feeling 'blue' meant.

And that's when he said, 'I couldnae be a painter. Shapes I get. I'm fine with them. But colours? Naw. I'm the equivalent with colours of what people with dyslexia are with words.'

And I said, 'You mean you're colour-blind.'

And he said, 'Naw. It's no like that. I mean, if two colours go together either in harmony or as a contrast, I'll unerringly choose a second colour that produces neither harmony nor contrast. All my art teachers have been like, "What is wrong with you?" I'm actually a wee bit better with words, though I'm pretty dyslexic too. But at least I understand words and make OK choices.

That's why I painted my mum's kitchen mustard. Because mustard. You know. That's like a food.'

And I said, 'So you didn't choose orange or tangerine? Hold on. You paint houses? You do decorating?'

And he said, 'Aye. How?'

And I said, 'The conceptual artist house-paints? I can see the headlines.'

And he said, 'Just for my mum.'

And I said, 'Yes, but. I mean, are you any good at it?'

And he said, 'Aye! Think I cannae paint?'

And I was like, 'Houses?'

And he was like, 'Aye.'

And I said, 'I'm sure you can house-paint.'

And he was like, 'Aye? Aye.'

I went on painting for a while and something was coming out of it. If I matched the colours of blue on his flesh to the paint on the canvas, something was coming out of it.

And then he seemed to be quietly laughing to himself and he said, 'Actually, that would be an interesting conceptual art project.'

And I said, 'What?'

And he said, 'An artist who house-paints as an artistic statement. And no even like painting art like murals, Alasdair Gray and the Chip and Bloomsbury folk doing their Bloomsbury houses or even CRM doing fancy-schmancy house décor as art and all that art deco malarkey. I mean like someone who paints three bedrooms magnolia. Ace, man. With nice edging. Or rubbish edging. Or a living room done with three walls Anaglypta and an accent wall in purple with purple skirting and a dado. As an art statement. See what I'm saying? What do you think?'

And I said, 'Aubergine.'

And he said, 'Eh?'

And I said, 'Not purple. Aubergine. It's a colour and a food.'

And he said, 'We're talking a living room, here, no a dining room. No foods-that-are-colours necessary.'

I was laughing really hard, but all I said was, 'Don't move out of position!'

And he said, 'Move? I cannae move.'

It was the first time he made me really laugh, like throw-your-head-back-showing-off-what's-up-your-nostrils laugh. And mibby it was the first time I got that he was into concepts of art like pushing at the boundaries of art or even that I mibby got what conceptual art was all about at all. I kept giggling as I imagined his house-decorating project into being, more and more details of where he took it, the television coverage, the art prizes and huge prices, Anaglypta and purple accent walls in ever more huge gallery spaces. But then I thought about his actual work and I thought, no, there was nothing to him. And anyway, he was too good-looking to have anything to him. Good-looking folk like him are always full of nothing but getting to the best parties and into the best nightclubs and getting jobs up Queen Margaret Drive at the BBC. Good-looking folk.

And, as I was painting, he kind of went quiet for a really long time and then suddenly he puked and I thought, Oh God, I have actually poisoned him. Later he said it was something he ate. But how could that be? What I mean is that his staple diet when I first knew him, if you can call it a diet, was pizzas from the ThreeInOne at midnight or

39

pakora and sauce from the other place on Renfield Street. I mean, mibby a diet like he had was dicey, but what I'm saying is that it's fairly clear to me that I poisoned him. Paint can do that. Poison folk. Poison pronounced 'pussian' as folk say on the islands. Pussian as in rhymes with Prussian. As in rhymes with Prussian Blue. That's the way island folk go about talking.

I finished the canvas this time, at least, but it wasn't right, it needed a bit more… I don't know, but I had some idea of this blue crucified Christ emerging from darkness like it was the point at which the skies darkened as Jesus died and the sky was rent asunder, and mibby if I just reworked it this way and that way and add this and add this and more paint and more blue and more black and more of everything… so that about a week later all I was left with, with the addition of more and more varieties of blue and black to the canvas, what I thought of then was a sort of moonscape Rothko in blue and know now was more like a Richard Pousette-Dart. Some nice elements of sacred geometry, like all the paintings I was going to do in the coming years had. But, really, it was hopeless.

As hopeless as they seemed that time in the Chip, his pals were good for something, as it turned out. The day after me and Douglas had decided that if we were going to get anywhere with this painting we were going to have to get a wooden cross from somewhere to lie him on, a couple of his pals turned up in a flatbed truck from God only knows where with a bunch of railway sleepers from God knows where. I don't suspect they were previously owned by the pals or anyone they knew, if you catch my meaning.

I said to myself as they were carrying them into the studio, Here comes the comic relief. And I said to Douglas, '*Ciamar a tha thu?*'

And Douglas said, '*Tha mi gu math.*'

And one of the comic relief said, 'God, do you lot know Gaelic? Do you know Gaelic, Cody?'

And Douglas said, 'Just "*Tha mi gu math*" and after that I'm out.'

And one of them said, 'I know "*slàinte*". You know, cheers!'

And another one of them said, 'Ho! Half time. These sleepers are heavy as oacht.' But the pals were good about moving them this way and that on the ground according to what I said. And at one point one of them said, 'Don't you think we should make an upright structure and get Cody up on it? We could do it now.' He turned to one of his pals and shrugged and he was like, 'Helps both ways, din't it?'

And I said, 'He has to be in the same position for hours for me to be able to work, so stringing him up doesn't really seem like a plausible option. We could kill him.'

At which the pal started laughing and he said, 'Let's do it! Performance art, man! Gonnae?'

And Douglas said, 'Time for you lads to be leaving.'

And the other pal was like, 'Spoilsport,' doing a big boo-hoo frown.

And the first pal, he was like, 'Come on, man, gonnae? Punk rock, man.'

You should have seen the clothes on them in them days. They were like teenage exorcists buddying up with the guardians of space.

And Douglas was like, 'Get! Scram!' to them.

And the first pal said, 'Aye. All right. We were going.'

The other pal started bolting for the door and he was calling out, 'Flee!'

For a couple of hours we worked with Douglas spread out on the sleepers and me up on a wee scaffolding platform we had constructed so as I could lie flat with a board between me and Douglas on the floor and I could sketch like that.

So, anyway, Douglas after a while said he needed to move and I was like, 'Just give me a...'

And he said, 'Suse?'

And I was like not speaking and kept sketching because I was just about to get something about the tendons and arteries in his neck stretching and he said, 'Suse, I've really got to move, move about, at least.'

And I said, 'Just, if you could...' not ending any sentences that way you do when you're really distracted and everything.

And Douglas just went ahead and pulled his arms across his torso and he was stretching and making big 'Oooooh' sounds like it was a hellish big relief for him to stretch and move.

And I said, 'Oh for God's sake,' really hissing it out and totally losing the thing about the tendons and arteries and muscles in his neck and it all flowed out of me like a current in a river I was getting swept away on and that's when my wee started trickling out of me off the platform and my head was lolling forward and I was mumbling, 'Can you hear that... Can you hear that noise?'

And he said, 'What noise? Susan Alison?'

And then I was saying stuff, and I could hear myself saying stuff, could hear individual words, sometimes a phrase. About punk rock. Yes, punk rock. And something about the *grips*? And something about no pleasure, no pain. Did I hear the word *dilettantes*? Loveless manipulators? I was asking questions. Asking if you knew what I was talking about, as well you might. Asking if 'you', whoever 'you' was or is or are, ever felt like… well, I guess the way *I* was feeling. Just feeling nothing and wanting to. And I asked this 'you', whether he or she or they 'you', I was asking whether he, she or they understood me. I could hear something about young men who give… *something*… And something about energies, contempt, fear, satanism and elitism. And something being *rotten*, Johnny Rotten and rotten rock 'n' roll, blood and sweat and Sigmund Freud. Obviously. And I could hear myself saying something else about cold noise and trash genius, and I was saying something about music so powerful, beyond control. About music, fashion, hearts and souls, and about *time*.

That was what it was like, this thing that was happening to me. These happenings were like memories of the present, being experienced in the present. And like memories of the past, sometimes they were crystal clear to me and sometimes they were a mess of mangled this and that. I mean, *now* I know all this punk rock stuff is a memory-mangled version of the mishearing-mangled version of the edited version of Iggy Pop talking to interviewer Peter Gzowski, 'Captain Canada' himself, on the Canadian Broadcasting Corporation in 1977, which Mogwai put on the opening track of their second album, *Come On Die Young*, but I didn't know this

43

then. This's all stuff, all this 'how-I-know-this-stuff' stuff, that I'll explain when the time comes. Just be patient.

And Douglas said later that he was just lying there bending and stretching his knees up to his chin, just watching me and thinking there she goes again because he was too relieved to be able to care much that I was having another seizure or whatever it was I was having.

After that I slept for quite a while where I lay, he said. I think he called what he spent the time doing was squat thrusts. Said he learned to do them in secondary school PE for before they got their turn on the trampolines. Imagining him as a schoolboy was a curious thing as he told me about it. I hadn't really thought of him until then as a person who grew up to be him, such was the force of him being him as he was then.

Well, then a couple of months after his pals had carried in the sleepers, I asked him if he could get one of the pals back over because I wanted the configuration of them changed and Douglas said, 'We don't have to bother them. I can move what you need moving.' I looked at him for a minute and he was like, 'What?'

And I said, 'You're kidding. Right? Two of them were lumbering away like nobody's business and you think you can chuck those around like they're matchsticks?'

And he said, 'It's all a matter of using the weight against itself. Fulcrums and that. When you're moving a heavy wardrobe around a house and up the stair—'

And I was like, 'Hold it. You're a house-flitter now, are you?'

And he was like, 'I've done my share. Whenever my mum needed me. Or, you'll find out, a wee while after

44

graduating your pals get sick of living out of a rucksack and start accumulating stuff. I've moved a massive desk three times for one of my pals, including to the fourth floor of a tenement.'

And I said, 'OK. Let's see what you can do.'

So he went about moving a few of the sleepers, and I have to admit he was pretty good at getting them across the studio and up against the wall. I was going to get him to kind of slouch against them at an angle and I said, 'See the way that one is angled against the wall? Do you think you could get a cross-beam to sit on it long enough to nail it against the wall there?'

He stared at the space for a couple of minutes, then he stared at the smallest sleeper, which was still pretty big. And eventually he said, 'It's about getting it to the cross-beam and getting it stable. I reckon we get the wee one up on the platform first then haul it across the upright.'

God alone knows why we didn't think to nail the upright to the wall first then cross-beam it, but we didn't. After two attempts with the whole thing coming clattering down Douglas said he had another idea. And he said, 'I think if we can just get the wee beam over my shoulders with equal weight on either side, we'll know where the fulcrum is and then I can just ginger the cross-beam on top right where it needs to go.'

And I said, 'Who are you, Hercules?'

And he said, 'I think you're thinking of Atlas.'

And I said, 'Whoever. It's not you.'

And he said, 'The wee sleeper is just big enough to be awkward. It's no really that heavy, no if we balance it.'

And I said, 'It's your funeral.'

And he said, 'Right. Decided. We'll get the wee sleeper up on the platform. You slide it forward on to my shoulders then I'll get up there and ginger it right on there.'

So I unlocked the wheels of the platform so we could move it out from where it was near the wall. Together we could just about lift the weight of the wee sleeper on to the platform, though I'm sure I was putting all the work in just because the difference in physique between Douglas and me meant all the weight seemed to tip to me. Then he squatted down at the platform and he said, 'OK, I'm ready. Hold on.' He put a rag over his naked shoulders and then he said, 'Right. That's me ready for definite now.'

I slid the sleeper from one side then the other and it was on Douglas's shoulders. The sleeper was kind of swaying from side to side like the wings of a plane taking off in a crosswind, but only a wee bit, and suddenly he was standing really still, legs in position like a weightlifter and the sleeper swaying came to a halt. And, straining, he was like, 'Right. Right. Move the platform there.'

I moved the platform back over to near the wall, where the upright was and locked it. Then I put the little step-ladder I had against it and moved away from there. Keeping the sleeper as still as possible, Douglas started a slow, slow rotation round to face the platform. And he kept saying, 'Right. OK. Right. OK.'

And I was like, 'Are you? Are you OK?'

He lifted his eyes from a head-bent concentration just long enough to sort of nod at me. Sweat covered his brow and I said, 'This's great. I need a sketch pad.'

46

And he was like, 'No! No.' His brow creased. And he was like, 'No time.'

For a second I lifted my hands to under the sleeper either side of his head as if I was spotting him. Then I thought, who am I kidding, I couldn't do anything for him this way, anyway, and instinctively, though he had said in no uncertain terms it could not happen, I looked round for a sketch pad. It was just something to do, I think. Now he was facing the platform he took a step, then another. Man, talk about a cross to bear. It made me think that if the real Jesus was supposed to have carried something like this all the way up a mountain or a hill or whatever it was, could that really be right that he did?

Douglas was at the bottom of the stepladder. And he was like, 'Wee bit closer.' Then he flicked his eyebrows. He wanted the platform closer to the wall. I unlocked it and pushed it hard up against the upright then moved the stepladder about a step away from Douglas towards the platform. He made a sound like 'Hnnn' – the sort of noise you make when you're just about to burst out crying, like this additional step to the stepladder was the last straw. Then he stepped forward and after a big, big pause he lifted his right foot to the first step, then after another big, big pause he lifted his left foot to the same step in a quick, jerky movement.

And I was like, 'OK. Just have to repeat that three times and you're there.' And somehow I knew he was reacting to what I had just said by the way his shoulders and head didn't move (I know this doesn't really make sense). Then he was on the platform and he and the sleeper seemed to just be still except for a kind of wobble that seemed to be more the air moving than him and the wood. Wobble. The air around him. And again he was still, but I knew he was preparing to lean forward and try to place the cross-beam at the fulcrum. Then he hesitated. I think he was seeing the impossibility of dipping his head low enough to get below the placing of the cross-beam on the upright and contemplating the impossibility of rotating so that he could lean back to the wall then squat down to the placement.

He began to lean forward and that's when the unlocked wheels of the platform felt the gravitational reality of the sleeper moving forward and down and rolled in acceleration towards me, toppling the stepladder in the process. And there wasn't a sound from Douglas as he fell like a dead weight and then a sort of crack noise followed by a crack, crack noise as his head hit the ground and then the sleeper hit his right shoulder, breaking a collar bone and splintering his shoulder blade.

After the ambulance ride, I had time in A&E Waiting to reflect on the utter stupidity of what we had done. When it healed his shoulder would for ever have a peculiar dent in it and his right arm always moved in a curious way at the shoulder. Douglas didn't get the same chance to reflect on our stupidity, because for ever after the effect only showed on his body and he had no memory of what we had done at all.

IV

We were down in London at the start of 1991. Douglas
had been shortlisted for the Turner Prize of 1990,
which was finally being awarded after a delay due to
some sponsorship snafu. He asked me to go along
with him. He didn't think he had a chance, and to be
honest neither did I. I didn't even have a clue why he
was on the shortlist. I mean, before Damien Hirst? Or
Gillian Wearing? Or Rachel Whiteread, or Chris Ofili,
or Martin Creed? Or Tracey Emin? Wait. Did she
win the year of *My Bed*? Or Douglas Gordon or Steve
McQueen? Or Antony Gormley? And you could tell
Douglas was nervous about it. When he was told by a
Glasgow Herald journalist on his doorstep that he'd been
shortlisted, the journalist said his reaction was to say,
'Not yet.' Too right. I think that was why he'd asked me
to go along instead of the comic-relief boys. If he still
had to go team-handed, the team was just me and him
now. He couldn't stand the idea that his *SIX WEEKS:
BLADDER INFECTION*, a large plastic bag filled with
blood-flecked urine, would look totally outclassed by the
other shortlisted artists' efforts. Somehow I think he felt

it would be better to bury his head into my shoulder when the catastrophe struck.

And then he goes and wins it. The look on my face was only surpassed by the look on his. I mean, deer in head-lights just doesn't come close. Then there was his drunken appearance on television that evening. I won't go into all that. This's all stuff of public record that you know already. The next morning, when I went to his hotel room to get him up, he had sort of slumped into a kind of depression, you would call it. But it didn't last that long when we got on the tube and headed off to the South London Gallery for the other thing we were in London for. As soon as we saw the exhibition there, Bill Viola's *The Passing*, the *Nantes Triptych*, well, it was like a resurrection. I mean, both of us were just awestruck and Douglas kept saying, 'Why have I stuck myself with this plastic urine bag thing when where it's really at is video art? This guy's a genius.'

And I said, 'Really, video?' But I have to admit, after an hour or so in with Viola's work, after I had gotten used to the audacity of the intrusion, Viola's exploitation of his own mother, I was pretty much thinking the same thing. When his mother died and the baby was born. 'Here's your baby, here's your baby.' Why was I bothering with paint when Bill Viola was doing what he was doing with video? Douglas wasn't wrong on that. When it struck me that my own mithair, and all mothers, and all of us would die, but we had been born, that was the thing, the miracle, I was in tears, because of the way it reminded me of my mithair. When Douglas caught sight of me, and I must have looked an absolute, utter, total sight, in pieces really, he reached out and pulled me towards him, curled up to rest his head on top of my head and engulfed me in his warm, beautiful arms and body. And he was like, 'Hey, c'mon, now. Hey. Hey.'

After I had mumbled a jumbled version of what I was thinking about mothers and dying and being born and miracles he held me even tighter. And he said, 'Every one of us alive is also dying, and one day we'll be dead, and every one of us who is dead is alive, in the memories of the living.' It seemed a strange sort of consoling, but it also seemed to make sense and I did feel consoled. It seemed nice to be reminded.

That reminds me that I keep forgetting to mention things about Douglas. Like, for example, his urine art wasn't his only project through these years. Though mostly known for the bags in his early career, he had the *1% OF MONSTER* thing, though really that was a collaboration, and then there was his later work, like my favourite, *WHAT LED TO MY CONSUMPTION*, which was a huge jewel-encrusted ashtray which, in the course of a year, he filled with every single smoke butt he discarded when in range of this ashtray. After that, he did *WHAT LED TO MY CONSUMPTION II*, which was this massive jewel-encrusted wine glass that he filled with an equivalent glass of wine to each one he consumed throughout a year. Then there was *WHAT LED TO MY CONSUMPTION III*, which was just the same deal except a huge (and I mean huge) jewel-encrusted pint glass filled with the equivalent glasses of beer to the ones he consumed over a year.

What else? Oh, yes, he could drive and had a car. I know! Who would have thought? He never drove it much, I'll give you that. Sometimes the facts come at you so fast it's difficult to know what to believe in. But he did drive. He drove us over to Garrowhill on the Easter bank-holiday weekend. He wanted to tell his mother face to face about the Turner Prize stuff. It was a peace offering of sorts because he had annoyed her lately.

I asked him how and he said, 'Uch, she was talking to me recently, asking me to remember some priest who was a chaplain at my school for a while, but I couldnae quite place him, and she was like, "Father Dolan, surely you remember Father Dolan?" And I was like, "Which one was he again, the drunk or the womaniser?"'

And I said, 'Ouch.'

And he said, 'I know. She wasnae speaking to me for quite a wee while.'

And I said, 'And you feel guilty about this?'

And he said, 'Whit? Naw. I don't feel guilty about it.'

And I was like, 'And you don't feel guilty about not feeling guilty?'

I suppose, when I think about it, he was leaning quite heavily on me around that time. And, since my Crucifixion was going nowhere fast, I was just happy to have any kind of distraction. I clocked just in time, before just walking straight into the hall like I would do at my mithair and faither's, that the brother who was opening the front door and the two sisters who were standing behind the brother were all not wearing shoes, and then Douglas was taking his shoes off and saying to me, 'You can leave them over there.' I looked over and there was a neat line-up of shoes of all sizes.

Then, when I hit the sofa, I naturally, like with my family, threw my left leg behind my right and landed down on my left foot and sat with my leg tucked up behind me and, this's the point, my foot on the sofa. Douglas and me and his mum talked for a wee while, but every so often she would sort of look to the side of me down at my left knee, sort of, and that's when I noticed that there were no other feet on furniture in the whole family, Douglas's, his mother's, his wee brothers' and sisters'. Feet were not on furniture. In my family home all feet would be on furniture.

And I was thinking, 'This's like how to be a werewolf. I'm Werewolf here in the home of the Dracula family, headed up by the friend of the night, no question.'

As I slowly tried to extricate my left leg and gently lower it to the floor, Douglas started talking about his latest discovery, and when he named and then described Andres Serrano's 1987 photograph *Immersion (Piss Christ)*, all I could do was look at his mother first to show my shock at this piece of art. But, then, when she didn't seem bothered at all about either the title or content of *Piss Christ*, the shock turned in on itself. My mithair would have hit the roof with this discussion. She'd have been like, 'Dear Lord!' Douglas's mother was sitting listening to him and every now and then asking questions or making comments which seemed to be trying to tease out of Douglas the meaning of this piece of art. Mibby that was what I was there to witness.

And then the mother was saying to me, 'What do you think, Susan Alison? Art like this is mibby not your kind of thing?'

And I said, 'Why is it that I'm thinking about that new work, Marc Quinn's *Self*, you know, the cast of his head made from his own blood? And, well, it does sound like this Serrano has some sort of...' and I was just about to say the word 'philosophy' when it struck me with unbelievable force that mibby it was just possible that Douglas had some sort of philosophical framework for his work. Honest to God, this had never struck me before, and it wasn't exactly making me happy.

Douglas's mum said, 'You're a painter, aren't you? Figurative, eh?'

And I said, 'When I'm working with Douglas.'

And she said, 'Oh? You do other works?'

And I said, 'Yes. Some other kinds of painting based on patterns and some work with fabrics.'

And Douglas said, 'Fabrics? First I'm hearing.'

And I said, 'They're not in the studio.'

The next time we were in the studio, his mind had obviously been whizzing about for ages because he had been silent and then he started speaking as though he was in the middle of his thoughts. And he said, 'Sometimes I wonder what would have happened if I had been sent to the Jesuits to be educated like my mother said she was going to.'

And I said, 'Hold on. Jesuit? That's the kind of Catholic you are?'

And he said, 'No. Dominican, actually. But those distinctions, you know, I'm not sure they matter.'

And I said, 'Dominican?'

And he said, 'It's all Catholic, really. What I was brought up in.'

And I said, 'I didn't think you were anything.'

And he was like, 'Thanks.'

And I said, 'Well, I don't think anyone is anything until I know they're something.'

And he was like, 'Your divine judgement, is it?'

And I said, 'You know what I mean. Normal. Like me.'

And he said, 'Naw. Brought up plain, simple, abnormal Catholic. And although you can say... You know, it's like that joke, "I'm an atheist", "Yes, but a Catholic atheist or a Protestant atheist?" You know what I mean? And what kind of Prod are you, anyways?'

And I was like, 'What do you mean?'

And he said, 'Well, you're a Prod, obviously, but there's different kinds.'

And I was like, 'How do you make that out?'

And he was like, 'You know. On the islands. There's all sorts. The Church of Scotland and the Free Church and the Wee Free Church and the Very Wee Frees and Wee Free Kings and—'

And I said, 'Are you insulting me?'

And he was like, 'Me? It was just a joke.'

And I said, 'Yes, well, can you make your jokes funny so I can identify them?'

And he was like, 'Aye, funny.'

And I said, 'And your mother was going to send you away to school? Priest school?'

And Douglas said, 'You didn't have to become a priest. It was just a school run by Jesuits. They were famous for their good education, especially in science. And I was showing an interest and aptitude in chemistry.'

And I said, 'Hold on. You were good at chemistry?'

And he said, 'Aye, inorganic chemistry. That was my favourite subject at school.'

And I was looking over at him and wasn't saying anything.

And he was like, 'Chemistry,' then he shrugged and then
he said, 'It was fun. Colours, explosions, fizzing and knowing how to explain it all.'

And I was like, 'Chemistry and Jesuits. Well.'

And he was like, 'Yup. Nut.'

And I said, 'Well, this will influence what the critics will
say when they analyse my Crucifixion.'

And he said, 'Oh, definitely.' And then he said, 'The
critics.'

And I was like, 'Are you mocking me?'

And he said, 'No, not at all. I think you have something.
Something.'

And I was like, 'Well, it's something more than a bag of
piss.'

And Douglas said, 'I won't even… Now I'm thinking,
I remember a story my mother told me. She was thirteen
or fourteen, and she decided she wanted to be a bride of
Christ, you know, a nun. She went to the Convent and
told them, "I want to be a nun." "Oh, how wonderful,"
said the Mother Superior, "a vocation!" She, my mother,
said that the Mother Superior then said my mother was
a little young, though, but to have a vocation at such a
young age was a wonderful thing. All she, the Mother
Superior, asked was that my mother wait just a short
time. She asked my mother to come back in a year, and
they set an appointment for her for one year hence. On
the anniversary my mother went to the Convent. "How
wonderful!" the Mother Superior said. "A true vocation!
How good to see you again!" And my mother talked about

wanting to be a nun, and found out more about the life of a bride of Christ.'

And I said, 'Bride... of Christ?'

And he said, 'That's what they call nuns. I think. They marry the Church. Well... So the Mother Superior, she says, "I ask only one thing of you, my child." That's the way nuns talk, according to her.'

And I was like, 'My child? Marry? *Marry* the Church?'

And he said, 'Aye. They all talk like that. She, the Mother Superior, says, "I ask that you come back in six months and tell me all about your hopes and fears for joining us in this life and tell me that you freely choose it." So my mother goes away again, and six months later she goes back. "How wonderful!" says the Mother Superior. And they talk half the day about my mother becoming a nun and all about nunning and what happens in the nunnery.'

And I said, 'Nunnery?'

And he said, 'Convent. Then, "Come back in three months, my child." And they talk for the whole day. Then the Mother Superior says, "Good. Come back in a month and we'll talk more." You must get the story by now.'

And I said, 'She didn't show?'

And he said, 'She'd met a boy.'

And I said, 'The nuns should have snaffled her up when they had the chance.'

And he said, 'Aye. Mibby.'

Mibby it's easy to see connections when you're looking back, like when people used to connect when I was first trying to paint my Crucifixion with it being the year that

Martin Scorsese's *The Last Temptation of Christ* came to the GFT. (That's the Glasgow Film Theatre, by the way, if you're unfamiliar with the details of Glasgow life. The GFT was just along from the Art School. Still is, as far as I know.) Anyway, I did probably see *The Last Temptation of Christ* at the GFT, but to my memory this would have been a revival showing, years after I had started trying to paint my Crucifixion. The GFT was great for revivals. Seeing films up on screen that you knew from the telly, like *Whistle Down the Wind*.

And none of this was as anything compared to 1973 or '74, primary school, and my teacher was into *Jesus Christ Superstar*. And she used to play the record to us, the original soundtrack.

There is a film I do remember seeing about the time, but no one ever mentions the influence of it on my painting. We were in line for tickets to the GFT to see a restored version of *The Gospel According to St Matthew*.

For a second Douglas looked sad. Or mibby he was just tired. His shoulders were hunched. And he said, 'I had a freaky experience at a party last weekend.'

And I was like, 'Do tell. Or mibby you shouldn't.'

And he said, 'It's not like any freaky party experience like you're thinking.'

And I said, 'Go on, then.'

And he was like, 'I ended up at this party…'

And I withheld a 'so far, so typical' comment.

And he said, 'Wasn't anybody's I know, we know. Don't really know how I ended up there.'

And I was like, 'Mhmm.' I was holding back about twenty things I could have said.

And Douglas said, 'And there was no drink nor nothing.'

And I was like, 'Eh?'

And he was like, 'They were, like, kind of a God Squad crowd.'

And I was like, 'Really. So it was a Jesus-freaky experience?'

And Douglas was like, 'Aye! Totally. I couldnae believe it.'

And I said, 'And you didn't just walk in and then out again?'

And he said, 'Something to do with the way not a one was drinking. It was so polite. You couldnae just, you know, "We are out of here!" And then I ended up talking to this girl… woman… Jesus-freak woman, you know.'

And I was like, 'Oh yes?'

And he said, 'It was nothing like that, believe me. So she's telling me how she thinks that Jesus would have definitely been a vegetarian, you know?'

And I was like, 'A vegetarian? Don't see much of that going on in Galilee in them days. Weren't they all sacrificing lambs and cooking them up for a good tuck-in?'

And he said, 'That's my impression, aye.'

And I said, 'Don't tell me – she was a vegetarian herself.'

And he said, 'You're way ahead of me. Though it only took her about three minutes to tell me she was and then tell me that I should be too.'

And I said, 'And a bit of Jesus worship from you too?'

And he was like, 'I think that was part of the deal, aye.'

And I said, 'I love that one. I've heard it before. My mother thinks Jesus was a knitter probably, because she likes a bit of a knit.'

And he said, 'Aye. Don't you think that Jesus was into horses? Because I just love my dobbin.'

And I was like, 'Yes, you've got it. Jesus, you know, he was probably a renowned tightrope walker. You know, because me, I just can't get enough of the old tightrope walking, and I feel so close to Jesus that we just must have that in common.'

And he was like, 'Aye. Jesus. If he were alive today, he'd be an HGV driver. Much as myself.'

We were pissing ourselves laughing by this stage.

And he was like, 'I seem to remember one of them had a mandolin, but none of them knew any mandolin numbers they wanted him to play, until one of them says they want to hear the *Bagpuss* theme tune. You know, that kiddie programme from the seventies. So the next thing is...'

And he couldn't finish for laughing so much. And then he was like, 'Next thing the conversation turns to something about religion, this being a God Squad party, you know, so me being a bit... anyway... next thing after the last next thing I'm like saying, "Well, to understand my point you'd really need to understand Spinoza." You know?'

And I said, 'How? I mean, what about Spinoza? Spinoza? You've read Spinoza?'

And he said, 'Aye, that'll be right!'

And I said, 'But, what were you on about?'

And he said, 'I don't know, do I? Next thing after the last two next things I'm talking to one of the other women and she's telling me how ridiculous it is that we're supposed to admire Burns as our national poet when he was a drunk, a fornicator and a wastrel. She actually used those words.

A drunk. A fornicator. And a wastrel. I didn't say to her, but her description made me interested in Burns for the first time in my life.'

And I said, 'So how long did it take you to finally get out of there?

And he said, 'Where?'

And I said, 'The God Squad party?'

And he said, 'Well, by that time I'd sobered up, hudn't I? So I just crashed out there to the sound of them all singing hymns or something. What? They were nice people.'

By this time we had tickets and were in a new queue into the screen. And I said, 'This's going to be great. It's the greatest film depiction of the life and death of Christ. It's pitch perfect, like when the wee light goes green on a guitar tuner.'

And he said, 'Aye? What do you know about guitar tuners?'

I ignored that and I said, 'It's by the poet Pier Paolo Pasolini.'

And Douglas said, 'The poet Pier Paolo Pasolini? That poet? Pier Paolo Pasolini the poet?'

And I was like, 'Leave it.'

Which he didn't, and he added, 'Is it perfect, this depiction by the poet Pier Paolo Pasolini?'

And I was like, 'I'd really leave it if you know what's good for you.'

And after he obviously searched around for another word starting with pee or a word with pee prevalent in it, which I could tell he was doing by the stupit look on his face, he finally said, 'Impossible perfection this depiction by the poet— Ah! That hurt!'

I had punched his arm with all the strength in me.

Whispering in the cinema, I said, 'What was that all about with your brothers and sisters all trooping off at one point saying they were going to do some praying? And then your mum going, too? What was that? Is that a normal Catholic thing? Doing that on a Tuesday?'

And he was like, 'No, it's not a normal Catholic thing. I mean, you get daily communicants, people who go to the church every day. But, anyway, that's Church and Catholics. To be honest, my mum and the brothers and sisters have become Rosicrucians.'

And I was like 'Rosy who?'

And Douglas said, 'Thy holy rosy cross. Rosicrucians. It's a kind of Catholic mysticism thing. And Rosicrucians, they believe there is a secret meaning, a secret code or something, and the Order of the Rosy Cross is a secret society from the middle ages.'

And I said, 'And what is it they believe?'

And Douglas said, 'I'm not really sure. I'm not in on it. Things like the secrets of Fátima and stuff, I think. Our Lady of the Holy Rosy Cross of Fátima. It's all about, I don't know, how the Pope knows when the end of the world's coming and stuff like that. Secret stuff.'

And I was staring at the side of his head as he stared at the screen. Then he looked sideways at me and he was like, 'I know. Look, that's them. I'm me. I know how this stuff sounds.'

And I was like, 'They sound like nuts. And with it being the bunch of them, it's like… it's like a mass-hysteria thing or something.'

And he said, 'Mibby it is.'

And I said, 'So you agree with me? Your family have gone nutty. Delusional.'

And he said, 'Well… You have to understand. This all got going after my dad died.'

And I said, 'Oh. Sorry. OK. A wee bit more understandable.'

And he was like, 'See? And, anyway, show me the difference between a delusion and a sincerely held religious conviction and then I'll be able to… Anyway. It doesn't really matter, does it? If it makes sense somehow that way.'

And I said, 'What was it your dad died of?'

And Douglas glanced at me and said, 'A kidney infection. His kidneys failed. Basically, one day he couldn't piss and the next day he was dead. Well, mibby he lasted a week. It's just facts, you know.'

When he told me more about it, his family's beliefs, it was all a lazy sort of Gnostic, Rosicrucian, Kabbalah mix and match where all that was really important was that they somehow knew something that was going on that you didn't. I mean, it was hardly Theosophy. As long as it was a secret religious experience, a secret religion, that was what was the central thing.

And I was thinking about how, when it came to be dinner time and the family was sitting up at the dining table and Douglas had said we would just eat where we were on the couch, what with there being no room for us at the dinner table, his mother said, 'You will not – they'll soon be finished,' and she kind of shoved two of the younger ones off their seats as they tried to bolt the last few mouthfuls they had. And then she said, 'You'll sit up like Christians.'

I turned to watch *The Gospel According to St Matthew*. Jesus was being crucified and night was falling.

The night that I remember clearest in 1991 was the night of the last day of the year and the New Year party that tipped us into 1992. It was in the Clevedon Crescent Lane garden flat of some bunch of geeks who thought they were cool because they had got their rave theme together by hiring a strobe light and who were playing *Screamadelica* repeatedly. The strobe was giving everyone headaches. And during all the jerky strobed movements of everyone, at the cool centre of all this, I found Douglas saying to one of the other boys there, 'Your name's Douglas? My name's Douglas.'

And this other Douglas said, 'Aw aye? Amazing. We can be like twins, mirror images of each other, eh?'

And our Douglas said, 'Aye, amazing.'

I reckon they were speeding. They had that look about them.

They kept on talking for a while and they were setting out their plans for domination of the art world. Our Douglas was telling the other Douglas about *THREE HUNDRED AND SIXTY FIVE DAYS*, asking him to estimate how big a vessel he would need to hold that much urine. The other Douglas was laughing and saying that as soon as he got the chance he was going to 'Write a short novel and make a record and a film.'

And our Douglas said, 'What abouts?'

And the other Douglas said, 'Well, I'm thinking of one film that's going to be abouts twenty-four hours long.'

And I said, 'Take a while to shoot.'

And the other Douglas said, 'No time at all.'

And our Douglas said, 'How comes?'

And the other Douglas said, 'I'll take a film and slow it down to play twenty-four hours.'

And our Douglas was like, 'Aye?'

And the other Douglas said, 'Aye.'

And our Douglas said, 'What were you thinking?'

And the other Douglas said, 'What was I thinking? Was thinking mibby *Psycho*. Hitchcock's *Psycho*.'

And our Douglas was like, 'Aye?'

And the other Douglas said, 'Aye.'

I can't remember completely what happened next, but there was definitely the sound of doors slamming and a wall being punched and next I'm on the doorstep of a tenement with Douglas, our Douglas, who is throwing up all over the pavement, shoulders hunched and heaving, and between gasps of breath and heaves he said, 'He's going to... be famouser... than me... and you... and all of us...'

And I said, 'So what? You just won the Turner!'

And Douglas said, 'He's down at the Slade now. London.'

And I was like, 'Aye, so?'

And our Douglas said, 'You heard his idea. A film you have to stand in front of for twenty-four hours? He'll be in Paris and Frankfurt and Berlin and... oh God... New York.'

And I was like, 'So?'

And he said, 'Because it matters.' It was the first time I had ever thought of Douglas – my Douglas, not the other one, who was Douglas Gordon if you don't know his work

– taking art, his art, totally and utterly seriously. He heaved again but nothing came up and he just spat out the bleurgh that was in his mouth and nose.

And I said, 'God, you're like a little boy sometimes.'

And he said, 'Heh.'

And I said, 'I mean, you're all like little boys sometimes.'

And he said, 'Thought you hated that, anyway, because of that time at school, when you were down behind the huts?'

And I said, 'What? What do you mean?'

But he didn't answer for a while, and was just staring drunkly at the ground.

And he said, 'Christ. I'm supposed to be at my mother's the morra for another New Year party. I'm supposed to first-foot her.'

He heaved for the last time, but there was nothing more to come up.

V

After a New Year like that, it was time to get back to work with some sort of conviction. I had been back at Dalí's *Christ of St John of the Cross*, where I always went for renewed inspiration (just like Craigie Aitchison, *Christ of St John of the Cross* was and is my Urtext), and I was thinking that the most important feature of the painting is that in essence we are looking down upon Jesus and not up at him. Dalí had said that it was the view of God upon his son that we were being allowed access to. My plan was to get the cross horizontal but high-ish up, mibby six feet or so, and then paint from the point of view of above and just behind the top of the cross, so that the most prominent feature would be the outstretched arms and top of the head of Jesus. And for that I'd need the sleepers moved.

I was telling him my new idea and I said to Douglas, 'Get in touch with the comic relief. You're not moving anything on your own again.'

And he was like, 'The who?'

And I said, 'Your Tollcross pals. The comic relief.'

And Douglas said, 'Aw, them. Well, my arm's healed now.'

And I was like, 'No way. What about the neuropathy?' He had been experiencing hellish pain deep down in his shoulder at his neck.

And he was like, 'Don't worry. It won't be like the last time. I'll get one of the boys over. I'm no daft.'

And as he headed for the door to round up one of them I said, 'Get that one with the huge shoulders.'

And he was like, 'Patrick?'

And I said, 'If that's his name.' I had by this time actually learned the pals' names and knew which was which and who was who. I don't really know why I put it this way. Just keeping my distance, mibby.

And Douglas said, 'Right. Tell you what. With the time it is now I'll head over to Tollcross and me and the boys were planning a night out at Bowsters and the Gandolfi, anyway. I'll head back here tomorrow with one of them rounded up.'

And I said, 'The one with the big shoulders.'

And he said, 'Patrick. Aye. OK.'

And so anyway, when he got back the next day with this Patrick in tow he said, 'You'll never believe the phone call I got.'

And this Patrick, he's like, 'Oor Douglas is going off to be a big star in New York.'

And I was like, 'What?'

And Douglas said to Patrick, 'Nice. Steal my thunder, man.'

And I said, 'What are you two on about?'

And Douglas said, 'I got a phone call. I've been invited to lecture on conceptual art at the New School in New York.'

And I said, 'What? For ever?'

And he said, 'A year. From May to next May.'

And Patrick, he was like, 'It has to be the Turner thing.'

And Douglas said, 'I suppose.'

And Patrick said, 'What else could it be? It's no as if you're that good a lecturer. Or any kind of lecturer at all. And your art is a loada pish.'

And Douglas was like, 'Aye? Funny man.'

And I said, 'A year?'

And Douglas said, 'Amazing, eh?'

And I said, 'Yes. I mean, aye. Yes. Amazing.'

And Douglas was like, 'OK. Do you want us to get these sleepers up where you want them, then?'

And I said, 'Is there a point, now?'

And Douglas said, 'How do you mean?'

And I said, 'Well, it looks as though I just lost my model for a year.'

And Douglas was like, 'Have you?'

And I said, 'Well, if you're going to be in New York, then yes, I have.'

And Douglas said, 'Have you?'

And I said, 'Aren't you listening? What is with you? Yes, I have.'

And that's when Douglas patted Patrick's shoulders and said, 'Have you? You said the most noticeable thing about him was his huge shoulders.'

And Patrick said, 'Eh? What?'

And Douglas said, 'Look at it this way. From the sketches you showed me it's no as if this next way you're doing is really going to feature much more than head and shoulders. And I think it's a brilliant point of view you're going for. It's like the God view, but as if God is falling off the edge of the world or something.'

And Patrick said, 'You want me to be the model?'

And Douglas was like, 'How no? This fits perfectly. Though, if this is the one that finally works out, I'll still be telling everyone that it's me in the painting.'

And I suppose I was thinking, 'This's never going to work out, but I am itching to try this point of view out now that I've thought of it.'

And Douglas was like, 'I'm no trying to play God here, but what do you think, Suse?'

And Patrick said, 'Do I get a say?'

And Douglas said, 'No.'

And Patrick laughed and said, 'Well, in that case, I'm in favour. Where do you want me?'

Me and Patrick. If you knew him – and if you're an art aficionado you might, because he's a moderately success-ful landscape painter now, but back then he made these stupit wee models of people being disembowelled and stuff like that, very Chapman Brothers, like an explosion in a tits factory, and he used to go on about his and Douglas's art having *affinities* – but I mean if you knew him *as a person* then you wouldn't exactly put us down as a marriage made in heaven. But Douglas got me to fall for the idea when he got Patrick to take his top off and pointed out that Patrick's arms look more like the arms on Christ in Dalí's painting than his own did. And my model was going to be in New York. If I wanted to keep working on my Crucifixion I really didn't have a choice.

Funny the wee things you remember. Like this conversation with me and Patrick.

He was rolling a smoke and I decided I wanted one but I don't really smoke. And so I said to him something I had heard someone else say, 'Can you roll me one, but just, you know, a skinny balinney.'

And Patrick was like, 'Eh? Do you mean a skinny Barlinnie?'

And I said, 'No, it's "skinny balinney". It just rhymes.'

And he said, 'Naw, it's no. It's because in HMP Barlinnie they have to smoke wee rollies because they don't have much baccy. They're on rations.'

And I said, 'Baccy?'

And he said, 'God, tobacco. Baccy. You don't know anything about this stuff, do you? You like to act rough tough Glasgow.'

And I was like, 'I don't know about baccy, no, but you're driving me batchy, that's for sure.'

And he said, 'Batchy?'

And I said, 'It's what my mithair would call it.'

And he was like, 'Batchy. Huh.'

And I said, 'Mental.'

And he was like, 'Batchy. Like mental. Huh.'

And I was like, 'So what if I don't know hard Glasgow facts? What's HMP, anyway?'

And he was like, 'Er, Her Majesty's Prison.'

And I said, 'Oh, yes, Barlinnie. I remember now.'

And Patrick was like, 'You need to spend more time in the East End, Susan Allson, down with us, around Tollcross.'

And I said, 'I've been to the Transmission a bazillion times. I am pure in there!'

And Patrick said, 'Aye. Good. You talk Glasgow. But you're not Glasgow.'

And I was like, 'What… an insult to come up with!'

And Patrick said, 'I'm no even sure you've ever been to an auld firm.'

That was about football in Glasgow, the derby game between Celtic and Rangers.

And I said, 'It's not necessary!'

And Patrick was like, 'It's just, I've known island girls before—'

And I was like 'Girls?!'

And he was like, 'And I've known ones that wanted to come see the footie but none that have ever changed their accents like you. Sheena.'

And I said, 'I haven't changed my accent. This's it. My family always had connections down here. And how many "island girls" have you known?'

And he was like, 'Well... two. But they were nothing like you.'

And all I could say was, 'Glad to hear it.'

And then Patrick said something he was to say a few times, a thing he never explained and which I did not like, which was, 'Hn. Douglas was right about you.' Sometimes he would say it as, 'Douglas is right about you.'

And I was like, 'What do you mean by *that*?!'

But he never answered. And it's funny what he said about me not knowing anything about HMP Barlinnie, considering.

Considering all this, when my mithair heard I was painting Patrick and not Douglas for the time being, she said, 'If you're painting another boy then why don't you do something different? Like your patron saint.'

And I was confused and was like, 'St Susan? Is there one? Or do you mean St Alison?'

And my mithair puffed and sighed and said, 'St Andrew. The Patron Saint of Scotland, so the patron saint of you and I and all of us.'

And I said, 'Oh, *that* patron saint.'

And she said, 'Well. You know, St Andrew didn't think it right, you know, to be crucified in the same way as our Lord. So he was still crucified, right enough, but he said, "No, not on an upright cross. Crucify me if you must, but hang me from a saltire cross." And that's what they did.'

And she wrote on a piece of paper in front of her:

not

And then she sat back and said, 'He was right to do that. He was penitent. A great penitent. And he asked that he be hung upside down, to be the opposite to our Lord. He was right in that also.'

And I said, 'Two rights, eh? Sounds like two rights make one wrong. Are you sure he was hung upside down?'

She eyed me suspiciously for a minute. And then she said, 'Wrong? Never. He was right. None of us are the Lord. And St Andrew, he was a pure soul.'

And I said, 'Because he suffered greatly?'

And she said, 'Exactly. He will be a very pure soul in heaven now, sitting at the right hand of the Father.'

And I said, 'I've been reading this good book on reincarnation.'

And she was like, 'About *what*? Isn't that some pagan or heathen thing? Reincarnation! Are you reading bad books? It sounds like a very bad book to me.'

And I said, 'What? Reincarnation is just like heaven, isn't it?'

And my mithair said, 'What *are* you talking about, Susan Alison? Nothing is *like* heaven because heaven is how close you are to God and to Jesus, your Lord and Saviour!'

And I said, 'Well, they're both about what happens to you after you die, aren't they? And about the soul and where the soul is.'

And she was like, '*What?*'

And I said, 'Heaven as a place where not you but your soul is.'

And she said, 'Not you? But your soul? You are your soul. At least, I am my soul and I hope that you are yours, too. Heavens above, Susan Alison, the ideas you have!'

And I said, 'But, I mean… Even the religions that believe in reincarnation don't believe you come back as yourself as a goat or a tree or a flea. You're not you being a cat or a dog or a wolf. You're not you somehow inside a wolf. You are the wolf, with no memory of your life before as a human.'

And she said, 'So in what way is that reincarnation, if there's not a soul, no you, being reincarnated? Ha. You can't answer that, can you?'

And I said, 'I can. It's because the you that's you is not the soul. The soul is something inside of you being a human, then when it's inside the wolf the soul is then a wolf. Do you see?'

And she said, 'I see that you seem to be saying something about werewolves, about how to be a werewolf. Is that what you're on about, Susan Alison? Witchcraft? Magick?'

And I was like, 'Oh, for God's sake, Mummy!'

And she screamed at me, 'Not the Lord's name!'

And I said, 'Oh, for… for the love of God!'

And she said, 'That's better. I think.'

74

And I said, 'And anyway, you're not supposed to believe there are witches and magick because you're a Christian, and Christianity banishes all that folkloric claptrap.'

And she was like 'Folkloric clap... *what*? Honestly, Susan Alison, sometimes I think you are a stubborn, stupid, idiot child. A wee bitty wired to the moon.'

Talking of idiot children, when I told Patrick about my mithair's idea he said he was into it, he got her point, that he couldn't think of a good depiction of Andrew as a suffering human being upon a cross. This was years and years before Peter Howson got round to doing one that was very much a suffering human. And Patrick said, 'Forget that hanging upside down malarkey. Your mother's just making that bit up, right? Isn't she?'

And I said, 'Yes, I think so. I'd never heard it before. I think she just got a wee bit carried away with the opposite-to-Jesus-on-the-cross idea.'

And Patrick said, 'I mean, hang me upside down if you want, I don't care.'

And I said, 'I think you would if I did that.'

And he said, 'Well, if it's just for a wee while, you taking a photo or whatever.'

And I said, 'No, me and Douglas work from first principles model-and-artist painting, so a sitting's a sitting.'

And Patrick was like, 'Aw, always old school? Fair enough, suppose.'

He got one of the Tollcross gang over and they moved the cross into saltire position, then Patrick just kind of stood on the ground with his ankles and wrists tied. I didn't think we could lift him off the ground. It would have ripped his body apart, surely. Would have made a hell of a suffering picture, though.

And as I was kneeling to tie his right ankle then his left, moving around down by his waist, Patrick started saying, 'Aye, I saw a film once with a guy in this position, though it wasnae for crucifixion purposes, if you know what I mean.'

And I said, 'You know, Patrick, I'm starting to get the impression I will always know what you mean whenever you're speaking to me.'

And he said, 'Aw aye?'

And I said, 'Rest assured.'

And he said, 'Aye, well, the guy in that film seemed to like it.'

And I said, 'I'm sure he did.'

And he said, 'Do you know Fiona Banner? Her work?'

And I said, 'No, who's she?'

And Patrick said, 'Oh, I met her at this Chapman Brothers thing in London. She's been experimenting with these... texts, long descriptions of films which she writes out and puts on canvas and up on the wall – you know, porno, eh, pornographic films, big long descriptions of them.'

And I said, 'Oh yes?'

And he said, 'Is that something... is that something that would interest you?

And I was like, 'Interest me? Get to France. What are you going on about, Patrick?'

And he moved along and said, 'You could always paint me like a man who is just dead.'

And I said, 'What's that?'

And he said, 'Well, you know, he goes stiff.'

And I said, 'Oh. Do you mean rigor mortis, Patrick?'

And he said, 'I'm sure you know what I mean, Suse.'

And I said, 'Yes, but doesn't that have to be a violent death?'

And he said, 'Does it? You sure?'

And I said, 'Yes. I mean, fairly sure.'

And he said, 'And crucifixion, that's not a violent death?'

And I said, 'Well, I mean sudden violence.'

And he said, 'And crucifixion is slow violence, eh?' He thought for a minute and then he said, 'Aye, actually, that sounds about right, slow violence.'

And I said, 'I'm not really just going for good old punch-in-the-face blasphemy, you know. And anyway, it's not new.'

And he was like, 'Eh?'

And I said, 'There are loads of fertility god statues with big stiff cocks, you know. And there's the big cock man at Cerne Abbas. I've been there.'

And he said, 'Aye, but it's no as though there's a big cock Jesus, is there? I mean, that would be blasphemy or something, wouldn't it?'

And I said, 'He was a man, not a bloody eunuch.'

And Patrick said, 'I always like him being called the lamb. The Lamb of God. I liked to think of him as a wee lamb. Anyway, who's painted him with a stiff?'

I riffled through a pile of art journals and pictures I had accumulated and showed him Kirov Tzucanari's *Jesus Dies on the Cross*. And I said, 'Have a look at this.'

He looked at the picture for a while, and then he said, 'OK. What is it I'm actually looking at here?'

I peeked over his shoulder and I said, 'Mibby it's not a very good reproduction.'

And he said, 'Of what?'

And I said, 'This's the painting by Kirov Tzucanari called *Jesus Dies on the Cross*. Look. More closely. There. What have we just been talking about? Look at Jesus just there.'

And he said, 'What? What am I looking for?'

And pointing I said, 'There. That. This's the painting where Jesus is reputed to have an erection under his cloth.'

And he said, 'Where?'

And I said, 'See this? This bulge in the cloth?'

And he said, 'Aw. Right. I see it now. It's a bit of an insult, isn't it?'

And I said, 'What, Jesus with an erection? A minute ago you were suggesting it.'

And he said, 'Naw. I mean, if that's supposed to be the size of it. I mean—' and he held up his pinky, then curled it. And he said, 'Not much.'

And I said, 'Well...'

And he said, 'I'd give you a bit more to paint if it was me.'

And I said, 'Oh, yes. I'm sure.'

And he said, 'That reminds me of a joke.'

And I said, 'I think we'll leave this one here.'

And he said, 'Really? I'll change the subject, shall I?'

And I said, 'That would come as a welcome relief.'

He thought for a second. Then he said, 'Have you ever heard of the Underground being called the Clockwork Orange?'

And I said, 'Me? No. Is it? How?'

And he said, 'Someone was saying to me it's been called the Clockwork Orange for years. You know, the trains are orange and the two circle routes going round and round like... clocks, I guess.'

And I said, 'Do you mean clock hands?'

He shrugged. And he said, 'Clockwise and anticlockwise routes.'

And I said, 'And this is a thing? This Clockwork Orange thing?'

And he said, 'Yes.'

And I said, 'I've never heard of that. I suppose if someone says it's a thing then it is a thing.'

And he said, 'I have heard of the Glasgow Underground.'

And I said, 'The trains?'

And he said, 'The, you know, the club, the music scene.'

And I said, 'Oh, that.'

And he said, 'Aye, you know. The Primaries. The Pastels. Dead and Dying Skateboarders. Phasers on Stun. Mayakovsky's Marvellous Half Moustache. The Shoplifters. The Submarines. The Artisans. The Duffles. All them bands.'

And I said, 'Oh, yes. I've heard of them bands.'

And he said, 'Aye?'

And he said, 'Play at the place down from the Equi and the place down by the River Kelvin just along from Kelvinbridge Underground. They call these clubs The Glasgow Underground. Tuesday nights the place down from the Equi and Friday nights the place down by the River Kelvin. You been?'

And I said, 'Yes. I just didn't know that was the name.'

And he said, 'Well. They keep it on the q.t., don't they? That is how hip we're talking. I mean, everyone's been – everyone's found themselves in these places at some point. After exams when we were students. And what else is there to do on a Tuesday night? All the artists have a place. All the people who don't have to get up on a Monday morning for a nine o'clock start. Them people. The artists. The bar staff. All them people. Not the street-sweepers. Doctors, nurses, clennie men. HGV drivers. The useful people. Not them. The other ones. Mostly the artists. There's a place that's the Sunday night place. The place you stagger from at three or four on Monday morning. That's called After Afterhours. From the song by the band – you know, from the lyric, "What happens after afterhours?" For the people who need after afterhours. Do you know that band The Ultramarines?'

And I said, 'You mean Submarines.'

And Patrick said, 'Naw. I mean The Ultramarines. They do songs about—'

And I said, 'Are they from Glasgow?'

And Patrick said, 'Bellshill. They do songs about cars, mostly. Traffic and that. Like their songs 'New Roundabout Ahead' and 'I'm Getting into My Car'.'

And I said, 'So?'

And Patrick said, 'So anyway, they do dae one song about, eh, a girl.'

And I said, 'Girl?'

And Patrick said, 'Aye. It's called 'Checkout Girl'. Goes…' and then he goes into singing this song:

Checkout Girl
Checkout Girl
You take my money and you change my world
Checkout Girl
Check out that girl
Whatcha got on under your overall?

And I said, 'It's a bit sexist. No?'

And he said, 'It's just one of those kind of songs, like 'Hello Baby, 'ave You Got the 'orn?'' He kept singing:

Checkout Girl
Whatcha got on under your overall?

And I said, 'OK, so what about it?'

And Patrick said, 'Well, the girl it's about, you know, I know her. I know who it was. I know who she is.'

And I said, 'Fascinating. Look, forget all that. Could you just take me somewhere nice tonight? Are you a dancer?'

It was the first time I had asked him to take me out and he said, 'Aye. Sure. Where to?'

'Where to' had also come up the night we got drunk together and somehow ended back at the flat he shared in the Gallowgate. I thought he had said party, but then when we got to his there were just his flatmates and a couple of others sitting around playing loud music and drinking and smoking but not much of anything else. Not what I'd call a party. Anyway, somehow we ended up just going into his room to hang out and talk. When we went into the room there was a bed without legs and a mattress on the floor, though everything was kind of neat and tidy and clean. Then I looked more closely at his bed as it seemed the only option for sitting down and I was like, 'What's *that*? Poking out from under your pillow, look.'

And Patrick was like, 'I think the question is, "Who's that?", you'll find.'

And I said, 'Who?'

And he said, 'That's Fitz.'

Fitz was a soft toy lamb.

81

And he said, 'I've had him since I was a wee boy.'

And I said, 'And keep him in your bed even now you're a big boy? Sweet.'

And he said, 'We've all got our wee… things?'

And I said, 'I suppose it's better than a knife or something.'

I suppose it was inevitable that Patrick was going to see one of my funny turns at some point. In fact, he seemed to be kind of waiting for it. He never said, but I suspect he had been briefed by Douglas. Still, when it happened he was a wee bit caught off guard. They're freaky that way. We were in the studio with the radio playing, which was unusual enough in itself. Patrick was waiting for some programme to come on Radio Clyde, where one of his mate's bands was going to get a play. Tracy Chapman's 'Fast Car' was on, I think. And this was one of the craziest to date. In two different voices, he told me, I started with, 'We gotta, we gotta do something about this.' And then I was like, in the other voice, 'When do you think you could make it over here? How long?' Then I was like, 'I could try and get there, about twenty-five minutes, maybe. Right. I'll try. OK. But we got to sort this out. OK. I'm just gonna go. I'm going to head off just now and try to speak to some people about this. Well, we've got to do something. Yes. Cause if we don't take care of this then… I don't even want to think about it.'

Then he said I was silent for a while, just humming some tune over and over and then I said in two other voices, 'Hello? Hi, Colin? Hiya. It's Martin. Hi Martin. I'm sorry to bother you. It's all right. But we've got a bit of a sketch going on here. What, what? Well, it's pretty hard to explain. So tell us, what? Right… we were down at Vic's and Stuart and Dominic got into a bit of a row. Mmhmm. And Stuart was getting a bit stroppy with Dominic and it ended up with Dominic punching Stuart and walking out… Mmhmm… Saying he's not coming back. Stuart's saying that he's out and stuff like that. Right. Stuart's away as well. Where's Stuart away to? He just phoned his dad and left. And is John still there? No, he went away with Stuart for some reason, to try and calm him down or something, it was a full bloody sketch, man, I don't know what to do, we've this thing on Tuesday. Right… kind of limited to what I can do, right? Yes, but me and Paul are here, totally, we don't know what to do, man, me and Paul are sitting here and we don't know what to do. Carry on mixing. Yes? This sort of stuff happened before, you know. It's pretty bad. It's just a 'kin' sketch. It's pretty bad. Erm, right, well, if you could give Stuart a phone, erm, we can sort something out, we'll just work around. We'll find out what it's about, I think Dominic's just gone to get wasted. Uh huh. Yes, but I don't know where he went, he just left, just went in the car and went. OK, well, I'll speak to Stuart, but then I'll get him to phone Dominic. Right, OK, fine, right, Colin, well, sorry to put a downer on your night. Fine, I'll soon phone you back. OK, no problem. See youse. Right. Bye, later. Bye.'

He said by the end he was just kind of wide-eyed, impressed with the performance sort of thing. And he was like, 'The tune sounded a bit like a Nick Drake tune.'

And I said, 'It's called 'Tracy'.'

And he was like, 'Is that a Nick Drake tune?'

And I was like, 'No.'

Apparently I was quite good at the different voices. Bouncing the sound around and that.

Sound was bouncing all around in this nightclub The Glasgow Underground he had taken me to a couple of months later, which was why he was screaming in my ear, 'EVERYONE HAS THEIR MOMENT TO BE GOLDEN, DON'T THEY? YOU COULD HAVE BEEN ONE OF THE TWENTY-YEAR-OLDS AT WOODSTOCK. OR AT THE NEWPORT FOLK AND JAZZ FESTIVAL THE DAY DYLAN WENT ELECTRIC AND PETE SEEGER WAS RUNNING AROUND WITH AN AXE SAYING HE WAS GOING TO AXE THE CABLES AND LEADS. OR, EVEN BETTER, THE NIGHT THAT DYLAN PLAYED THE MANCHESTER FREE TRADE HALL AND THE GUY SHOUTED OUT, "JUDAS!" "JUDAS!" YOU KNOW? THE GUY WHO SHOUTED OUT, EH, "JUDAS!" AND DYLAN WAS LIKE, "I DON'T BELIEVE YOU. YOU'RE A LIAR!" OR AT THE MANCHESTER LESSER FREE TRADE HALL WHEN THE SEX PISTOLS PLAYED. OR, YOU COULD HAVE BEEN AT THE EXPLODING PLASTIC INEVITABLE LISTENING TO THE VELVET UNDERGROUND PLAY SO LOUD AND CRAZY THAT YOU CANNOT THINK, JUST LIKE FOR ANDY. OR IN ZURICH AT THE CABARET VOLTAIRE THE NIGHT DADA WAS INVENTED. OR AT THE MERRY PRANK-STERS' FIRST ACID TEST. WATCHING ZIGGY KILL THE MAN AT THE HAMMERSMITH ODEON IN NINETEEN SEVENTY-THREE. IN THE CEDAR TAVERN IN NEW YORK IN NINETEEN THIRTY-SIX WHEN IT WAS ON FIFTY-FIVE WEST EIGHTH STREET. IN THE CHELSEA HOTEL WITH JANIS

AND LEONARD AND KRIS. IN THE CHATEAU MARMONT WITH ANYONE HAVING YOUR GOLDEN MOMENT. THERE, THEN, COULD BE YOUR TIME TO BE GOLDEN.'

I looked at him. I couldn't be bothered screaming back.

And he screamed on, 'OR... OTHER PLACES CAN PROVE TO BE GOLDEN THEMSELVES, PLACES TO BE GOLDEN IN. THOUGH WHO WOULD HAVE THOUGHT OUR TIME TO BE GOLDEN CAME IN THE NOTHING YEAR OF NINETEEN EIGHTY-SIX IN THE NOTHING PLACE OF A DANCE-ROUND-YOUR-HANDBAG NIGHTCLUB CALLED DADDY WARBUCKS? BUT THAT WAS WHERE WE WERE AND WE WERE GOLDEN IN OUR GOLDEN MOMENT, AT THE SPLASH ONE HAPPENINGS. I MEAN, JESUS GOD, WE GOT TO SEE THE SUBMARINES AND PRIMAL SCREAM AND THE SOUP DRAGONS AND THE PASTELS AND THE SHOP ASSISTANTS, BMX BANDITS AND SONIC YOUTH... I MEAN, SONIC YOUTH!'

A thought struck me, because even I knew those Splash One Happenings weren't on any more, to ask him where he and his music pals hung out now. But I still couldn't be bothered screaming. I imagined it was probably this place where we were, where on sad, dreich Monday nights his bedraggled troops would strum through songs about traffic and drizzle. Loud, quiet, loud, quiet, loud, louder, stop. Stuff like that. And he was shouting, 'SOMEWHERE RIGHT NOW SOME PEOPLE ARE HAVING THEIR GOLDEN MOMENT RIGHT NOW.'

And I said, though I didn't shout, so I was drowned out, 'Yes. Somewhere.'

And the funny thing was, not music- or nightclub-wise, but artistically, I was starting to feel I *was* in some sort of Golden Moment of my own. Douglas was in the moment, that's for sure. And even Patrick was there, too, then. And Stephen, remember Stephen from the start of this story? He was in the moment, too. He had got quite famous for his paintings by this stage, famous enough that I've changed his name.

Patrick had stopped shouting and was looking into the lights flashing, and the music that was playing was 'Come Together' by Primal Scream and out of the blue I was thinking, you know, mibby *we* are in love, but it's that kind of love, *amour fou*, *Betty Blue* kind of thing, or whathuvye – you know, 'I love you, I'm going to blow up your school' sort of dealio. I *know*, right? Me and *Patrick*! But keep your hair on. I found out years later he had slipped an E in my drink. It was those kinds of times.

It was all coming to an end for me and Patrick. Douglas was going to be back in my studio soon enough and the Crucifixion painting I was completing with Patrick, the St Andrew farrago, was well by the wayside by this point... Well, what can I tell you? Same deal as ever. I mean, a nice blue and black and red abstract, I thought, but an over-daubed abstract, none the less. Abstract expressionism. Jesus, even Rothko rejected the term. And what was it I was expressing, anyway?

I was thinking, 'Why does this always happen?' Anyway, I can tell you the way things finally ended between me and Patrick, because eventually, a couple of years after I first ever met him, it was like, not *you* again. And I said to him, 'Patrick, stop coming to my house.'

VI

Once, Patrick said, 'I like your idea about flesh. It makes me think of when I was eleven, mibby twelve, mibby thirteen, and Stevie and I would go to the only place we could see the thing that we were at the time most fascinated by, the flesh of girls. So we used to go to the public baths with our goggles and we would dive down, fully immersed, and look at the bodies of girls floating gently by in the water.'

And I said, 'Uh. Creepy.'

And he said, 'What, "creepy"? We were wee boys. We weren't doing it when we were twenty-year-olds. We just wanted to see the bodies of girls. And you couldnae just go staring at them above water, could you? I still say it's what made me good at my life drawing classes when I came to the Art School.'

And I said, 'Were you? I never knew that about you.'

And he said, 'Aw yes. What, you think it's... I've been thinking about bodies since I was born, about blood and tears and lymph and interstitial fluid and pus and pish. Did you think it came from nowhere?'

And I said, 'Well...'

And he said, 'You did, didn't you? *Don't* you? Jesus God. You thought I was just a wee bed-wetter turning the world on its head. Cheers. Thanks a lot.'

A lot of things had happened by the last times I hung out with Patrick. One day I idled a question at him, 'What's the most immoral sentence in the world, do you reckon?'

And he said, 'Eh, right. Erm. I think probably, "I love you and that's why I have to kill you." Dig it?'

And I said, 'I do. Good. But there's one step on from that one, I think. Check it. "Look what *you* are making *me* do to *you*." No?'

And he said, 'Eh.'

And I said, 'Come on. Get it. "Look what *you* are making *me* do to *you*." It's like, not only are you being punished or killed or starved or whatever, but it is also *your* fault this's happening to you. No?'

And Patrick said, 'Aye. OK. I get you.'

I just wanted to get back to the way things had been. What can I tell you? After the little Patrick interlude, I was happy when Douglas got back from New York. I don't think he was happy to be back, though. He seemed unsettled, like he wanted the rest of his career to happen right here, right now, to be jetting off all over the place and exhibiting his art everywhere that would exhibit it. But for the time being, by the end of May, he was back in Glasgow and I was happy to have him back. Even if it did mean having to sit through discussions like this one:

Douglas was talking about *Joe 90*, a television programme from his childhood, asking Patrick, who was a wee bit younger than him, if he had ever seen it.

And Patrick said, 'Oh aye. I think it must have had reruns going on through the nineteen seventies.'

And Douglas said, 'Aye? Aye, I suppose.'

And Patrick said, 'Aye, I liked it, though the plot always seemed to be—'

And Douglas was like, 'Driving a truck with loads of, loads of, like nitroglycerine—'

And Patrick was like, 'Aye, TNT and dynamite and stuff…'

And Douglas said, 'Aye, loads of dynamite in these… on these shaky shelfs or something…'

And Patrick said, 'Aye. Shaky. And the road up the mountain is really treacherous.'

And Douglas was like, 'Aye, really treacherous and bumpy, and the dynamite is like shaking about. Always that. Always.'

And Patrick was like, 'But old Joe, eh, he always gets to the top of the mountain or wherever without, you know, BOOM. He always—'

And Douglas said, 'Aye, he always made it. Was it… was it because he was so brainy or something? Is that what happened to him in the twirly thing he sat in?'

And Patrick was like, 'Aye, but being brainy? Is that what skills are needed for driving dynamite up mountains?'

And Douglas said, 'Was it…? Mibby he had… what would you say was his superpower, really?'

And Patrick said, 'Was it…? Was it…?'

And Douglas was like, 'I think it was that he had a HGV licence or… yeah, a—'

And Patrick said, 'Aye, heavy goods vehicle—'

And Douglas said, 'Aye, heavy goods… HGV licence—'

And then they were both laughing like drains, like giggling idiots. It was nice in its way to see them together.

But it felt better to get back to the conversations we – me and Douglas – had been having for years. One conversation in the Equi Coffee Bar on Sauchiehall Street sticks out for me, when Douglas spoke about a plastic crucifix he had above his bed when he was growing up and his mother having a Sacred Heart of Jesus and, once I understood what he was telling me, I said about wanting my Crucifixion to look more like these than the most searing, greatest depictions of the Crucifixion, what some would have thought of as the most – and I use the word advisedly – 'authentic'. I wasn't into authenticity. I mean, who even knew whether the crucifixion of a man called Jesus actually happened and what it looked like? But I did want my painting to be genuine. Genuine is better than authentic.

And I said to Douglas, 'Genuine is better than authentic. Don't you think?'

And he said, 'Eh? Aye. Me? Genuine. Definitely. How do you mean?'

And I said, 'What do you mean, how do I mean? Either you get what I'm saying or you don't.'

And he said, 'I do get it. Authentic. Genuine. I know the difference.'

And I said, 'You do, do you?'

And he said, 'Aye. Listen. When I was a wee boy my mother bought me this crucifix to put up on my wall above my bed. And it was… Well… It was plastic, for starters. About mibby this high.' He gestured with splayed thumb and index finger. And he said, 'And it… Well, it wasn't even a good plastic cast of Jesus. The facial features were especially bad. Just a kind of generic beardy man with dabs of red paint here and there. On his brow and his wrists and in his side and on his feet. A wee plastic thing it was. And what I'm saying is… Well, that crucifix with the generic Jesus on it was not a piece of authentic art. It wasn't a piece of art at all. It was as much art as the green oriental lady or a biscuit-tin Scottie dog. Meaning it wasn't authentic art. But it was sincere. The people who produced them were sincere people. They wanted wee boys and girls to have wee crucifixes with wee Jesuses on their bedroom walls. They thought that this would help these wee boys and girls be pious and holy or something and suffer the little children to come unto me. Naw? What I mean is, it was genuine, this wee plastic Jesus on a cross. There was something genuine about it. A genuine thought-and-feeling being… what's the word? Transmitted. Do you see what I'm saying?'

And I said, 'Yes, I get it.'

And he was like, 'Aye?'

And I said, 'Yes.'

And he said, 'Wee girls and wee boys being pious. Makes me want to heave. Heh, are you going to tell me your story about what happened at school down by the huts?'

And I said, 'No.'

And he said, 'Thought so. And she had this Sacred Heart, my mother. Do you know what they are?'

And I said, 'Not really.'

And he said, 'A picture of Jesus looking straight at you while his finger points to his chest, except it's not his naked chest you see or his clothes over his naked chest. It's actually inside you see his heart, though not an anatomically correct heart. More like a Valentine's Day card heart with light beams coming out from behind it, lighting up his whole chest and even the space around him. It represents—'

And I said, 'The soul?'

And he said, 'Aye. The soul. Or the divinity of him? Something like that, anyway.'

And I said, 'The God inside the man?'

And Douglas said, 'Aye. Aye. Something like that, anyway, and that. Anyway. My mother, she's like, "Look at the eyes, Douglas. Watch his eyes." And she would move the picture around a bit. Twisting it a wee bit back and forth in her hands. "Do you see the eyes?" she'd say. "Do you see the way they follow you around the room?" Kind of creeped me out a wee bit.'

And I said, 'What was her point, do you reckon?'

And he said, 'Aw, I don't know what to say. Probably something like the eyes of Jesus are always on you. It takes you somewhere and now you're taken. He is watching. From somewhere, and I guess she meant heaven, Jesus was looking down on all of us and knew what we were doing.'

And I said, 'To watch over us and protect us.'

And he was like, 'What? Are you kidding? Naw. Keeping an eye on all our filthy wee sins as we sinned them. Judging us. Being disappointed in us. Condemning us. Naw? Aye!'

And I said, 'Really? Jesus.'

And he was like, 'Aye!'

And I said, 'Your religion isn't very nice.'

And he said, 'And yours is?'

And I said, 'Yes, well, fair point. So who were the artists?'

And Douglas said, 'What artists?'

And I said, 'The artists who made the crucifix and who painted the Sacred Heart.'

And he said, 'There's no artists. Or there is but nobody cares. They probably knock these things up in the Vatican, making millions at a time. Get them out there and sold.'

And I said, 'The pieces aren't attributed to any artist?'

And he said, 'Not to my knowledge. That's what I mean. That's why I'm saying it isnae art at all. No artist, no art.'

And it reminds me now, that night, going to sleep, I heard this sound. A guitar or a bass guitar going dada dada daaaaadum and I could hear, 'Did you see him when I was away? I would have phoned... Will he be in the pub tonight? ...Take a sip. Will he be yours as of today? Will I never see you now you're taken? Are you still wearing that ring? ...Like a bird... Her sister says that we'll get wed. And I should tell you I adore you...'

And then I was asleep. I dreamed about Andy Warhol. He was telling me about the authenticity of cheap reproduction. He was with me but he was also on the phone to me, except I was not me.

Not for me, but for Douglas, I think, it had started to seem like it was going to be an awful long walk to Calvary. Well, mibby for me, too. Finally we had decided if I was going to paint a Crucifixion with any sense of a reality we could stand by, then it was time to get the comic relief back over to knock up an actual cross, an upright cross standing four square in the middle of the studio on which we would tie Douglas's arms and let his body strain as he hung there.

After his friends had left he said, 'Let's give it a go, then.'

And I said, 'Now?'

And he was like, 'Why no?'

And I said, 'Suppose.'

So we got the platform and I got up on my ladder – the full ladder, not the stepladder – and he stood on the platform as

I stood up at the cross-beam and tied his arms to it carefully, over and over.

Then the time came to move the platform away and let him dangle from the cross-beam and see whether the ties would hold. I mean, he wasn't that far off the ground, a couple of feet at most, so if the whole deal came crashing down there wouldn't be any major problem. But that's not the way it worked.

And I was like, 'Are you ready?' as I got back on the ground and prepared to move the platform from under him.

He sort of squirmed in the ties for a bit, getting as comfortable as he could, and then he said, 'Aye. All good. This should be no bother. I'm tied tight.'

And I said, 'Right, I'm going to push this away now. Are you ready?'

And Douglas said, 'Yes, do it.'

And I said, 'You're sure?' It didn't look right to me.

But Douglas was like, 'Do it, go on, do it quickly.'

And I said, 'Right, here goes.'

For a second I paused. What was it about the arrangement that looked wrong? And then I was like, 'OK, then,' and I just sort of shoved the platform away from beneath him.

As soon as this happened you could almost hear a sort of whiplash of the ties pulling tight beneath his elbow (I had tied them over and over, right up his arm) and his arms bowed back in an unnatural way, leaving his hands both spasmingly tight and yet limp. And the noise that Douglas was making – a sort of YES and NO at the same time... and then he was screaming, 'JESUS CHRIST!' and then more screaming, just a repeated animalistic, guttural sound like 'MUUH! MUUH! MUUH!' His legs and feet were twitching.

Of course, I was straight to the platform trying to get it back under him, but I was also trying to take in the sounds he was making and the look on his face, which burst into a curious sweat and vermillion and purple colours, and his legs and feet twitching. That twitching. I had to remember this, the way the muscles spasmed and twitched. And he had reached 'FUH! FUH! FUH!' when I finally got the platform back under his feet, though even these were twitching so badly I had to physically lay them flat on the platform base and hold them till they stopped and became still.

Still, later on he said, 'We just need a better way of doing it. And I tell you what, I'll get my camera and you can take a photo of me. You can let me scream for as long as it takes to take the photo. Deal?'

I know, I know. Obvious, right? Really, I wondered why it had taken him so long to figure this out, and wondered why it hadn't struck me as a way forward at all. Mibby we were both just so into suffering for art.

And when we did it, the photograph, there was just something so compelling about the look on his face as he struggled to keep himself on the cross that I had to do something with it. As I mentioned, the other big thing I was doing other than painting at the time was work with fabrics, the draping and hanging of rich fabrics and intricate embroidery work that was costing me more time than it was really worth, but that photograph made me think. I had to do something in fabric with the image of his face in torment. It would just be so beautiful, and, one day, I'd think of the eventual work I made as the best work I had ever done.

One day, as I looked at him and noticed that, though he had always been slim, he was looking thinner than I had ever seen him before – like Bobby Gillespie, mental thin, skin and bone, really, like a lanky streak of piss, as my faither would say – I said something about him being a six-footer and that he couldn't afford to be losing any more weight. And Douglas was like, 'You know, when I was wee, I was wee.'

And I said, 'Six-footer like you?'

And he said, 'Aye. I was always getting battered at a scramble.'

And I was like, 'You're kidding. No?'

And he was like, 'Aye. I mean, no. All the noise and that, the scramble getting going and then a kick in my phiz and the noise all went loud. All battling in my bonce. Going mental and I'd be down. Then I'd come to and nothing. Nothing to show for the scramble.'

And I said, 'That… probably inhibits your confidence.'

And he said, 'Aye? Aye. Well, I was a target. I stayed in too much, didnae play football with the other wee boys.'

And I said, 'Awww. Wee man!'

And he was like, 'Aye, all right, all right. No need to… It was just that after I had shown what I could do my mother was always like, you know, practice, practice, practice!'

And I was like, 'How do you mean, what you could do?'

And he said, 'Oh, did I no mention before?'

And I was like, 'What?'

And he said, 'Just, you know, I showed early promise. My drawings. I used to do pencil drawings that were pretty good. Accurate, I mean.'

And I said, 'How good are we talking, here?'

And he said, 'Well, I don't know what to say... Good, I guess.' He paused. And he goes, 'Got me into the local press good. That sort of thing.'

And I said, 'What? What kind of age were you?'

And he said, 'Eh, I don't know — four, mibby? They called me this thing...'

And I was like, 'Four? Four!'

And he said, 'Older than four, mibby. Like I said, it was this wee show of talent, of promise. I mean, it never added up to much.'

And I said, 'Well, it got you into the local paper.'

And he said, 'Aye, that. When *The Times* picked up on it, though, I thought things were going a bit too far, you know?'

And I said, 'National press? You were that good? At four years old? And *The Times* did a story on you?'

And he said, 'Aye. That. And remember that TV programme *Nationwide*? I was a... what's the word? They called me something on *Nationwide*.'

And I was like, 'You were on *Nationwide*?'

And he said, 'Aye, well, they were always scouting for these wee local stories to go big on them, weren't they?'

And I said, 'My God, you were like some sort of child prodigy.'

And he was like, 'That's it! That's the word they used. On *Nationwide*. "Prodigy." "You've heard of Mozart..." they kicked off with.'

And I said, 'I can't believe it.'

And he said, 'Oh, I suppose I was always good at drawing. That's why I couldn't really be bothered with it. It was like performing-seal time.' And he slapped his hands together and made a sound like 'Uhp uhp uhp'. For a moment he looked broken by the memory.

And I said, 'For a wee while when I was wee I thought Father Christmas was the father of Jesus.'

And Douglas said, 'Father Christ. Mass. Can see it.'

And I said, 'Yes? I suppose.'

And then he said, 'By the time I was ten I was refusing to draw anything. Even for my aunties and uncles. Even if they were offering sweeties and I was starving for them.'

We were starving and he talked me into heading round to The Ubiquitous Chip for something to eat. I had a big 'hungry' face on, I guess.

And I said, 'How will we afford it?'

And he was like, 'Artists don't care about that stuff. Anyway. I have ways. They know me there.'

I was so hungry I didn't ask any more questions.

We got there and Ronnie the owner greeted Douglas by name. I thought this was a good sign. Then Douglas nodded at the murals on the wall. And he said, 'Alasdair Gray. He does all the art in here.'

We were sat in the best seats. Downstairs in the former courtyard of whatever this place used to be. It was all big plants and a pond with tinkling water flowing. I was in awe of the flagstones. I know that sounds daft, but you should see the flagstones in there.

We ate unbelievable food and drank their best wines. All hugely expensive. For Glasgow, anyway. Mibby for anywhere. Then it came time to pay the bill. Ronnie the owner came over to the table just before we'd finished and said we should go up the bar and then everything could be settled up. We went up there and I had a glass of champagne and Douglas had a beer.

And about an hour later Douglas said 'I have to go settle the bill. I'll be back in a minute.' He left me for about fifteen minutes or more. I got antsy and at one point I went over and looked down at the courtyard. Down there I could see that Douglas and Ronnie were talking. God knows what abouts. But at the end of their conversation they shook hands and when Douglas came back up to the bar he said the bill was settled.

And I said, 'What's gone on?'

And Douglas said, 'Nothing. But have as many drinks at the bar as you want. It's covered.'

And I was like, 'What's going on?'

And Douglas said 'Nothing. Just Ronnie likes my art and we can have as much to drink here as we want. See the murals? Alasdair's murals? He did those and Ronnie fed him for the bother.'

And I said 'And it's the same for you, is it?'

And he said, 'What? Naw. That's just… Alasdair is one of Ronnie's old pals. But yes, he will support young artists like me and you.'

And I said, 'Me? He doesn't know me.'

And Douglas said, 'You're with me.'

And I said, 'And that's enough, is it?'

And he said, 'Look, we're good here. Isn't that enough for you?'

And I said, 'Suppose.'

And he said, 'I'd hope so.'

And I said, 'But why did he let us off the bill? What did you give or promise?'

And Douglas said, 'I like your questions. Keep asking. That's why I like your quest for your Crucifixion.'

And I said, 'Yes?'

And he was like, 'Oh aye. Look, don't worry about the food. You can get it next time, OK?'

The next time we were heading out from the studio for a drink he annoyed me, and I mean really annoyed me, when he said about us going to the Park Bar and I said, 'What? Why? Because I'm from the island?'

And he said, 'No, just because it's close by.'

I knew he was just lying, and it was because I'm from the island that he said the Park Bar, I know it. And then there was the time he said it was whisky time. And I said, 'Excuse *me*, I *never* drink whisky!'

There were getting to be more of those days, to be honest. Remember the day, we've all been there, the day you got drunk all day? Something accidental means you start early and then it never seems to stop – you're just going to be on the rollercoaster of being drunk and crazy and you're going to have to accept that that's that. Till the crash comes. But I remember just before the that's that that I said to Douglas, 'Of course, it's you that I'm getting drunk and crazy with, of course it is – I think we need to string you up properly, my boy,' kind of kidding, kind of. He took it in good part.

And he said, 'Aye, I get your point. My muscles just won't flex the way you want till they're, you know, till there's duress, and for an extended period of time, till I'm enduring something. That's the way it would have been for him.'

And I said, 'Who?'

And he said, 'Eh, Jesus, like. You know, your man.'

And I said, 'Oh, yes, of course, Jesus.'

By the end of that session I was, you know, as my mithair would have been black affronted to say, two sheets to the wind — I couldnae bite my own finger, I was so out of my teeth.

The next few days were a bit of a blur, but there was a night bus to London, and walking around in a hung-over daze trying to find somewhere to eat breakfast and then standing in front of the painting *Wine Crucifix* by Arnulf Rainer in the Tate, and I said, 'That's just how my head feels.'

And Douglas was like, 'I just feel totally fat, man. Fat head, man. That's me.'

All I could do was sigh and hold my head in my hands. I felt like we were on the high seas and my body kept moving up and down on these huge waves. It seemed like days rather than hours after we had got on the bus, with him shouting all sorts of rubbish at the driver and everyone on the bus. When he had been like, 'Wahoohoo! Giddy up! Devil rides! I want close encounters!' Utterly pished.

And then Douglas said, 'I'm moving here.'

And I said, 'Where?'

And he said, 'London. Somewhere around Hoxton, Clerkenwell. Or Shoreditch.'

And I said, 'You're serious.'

And he said, 'Never been more.'

And I said, 'But, why?'

And he was like, 'Have you got the picture of what the art scene round there is like? I just don't feel I can... I can come back from New York to... I don't know what to say... Glasgow. Know what I mean?'

And I was about to say, 'No. You're part of the Glasgow scene, you're part of what makes Glasgow a vibrant art scene, you can't just walk out on... it.' But what I actually said was, 'Yes.'

And he said, 'And anyway, while I was away the guy who was flat-sitting for me, he taped over my Luis Buñuel films that I had on VHS, taped over them with an auld firm match. Know what I mean, man? I just knew then. I had to move to London. It's just in the ether, man. I cannae take this ether any more.'

He started making preparations to move all his stuff to London, sell up his flat and find a studio down there. I suppose mibby you're going to say something psychological about how the move to London was about the same time I had started binding him physically to the cross. But I'm not sure you're not making too big a deal of this. Or mibby you're not. I guess who am I to say? Read it any way you like.

So, anyway, the painting didn't work out. But there was the photograph of him, of his face, and I didn't tell him about it but I was working away on the embroidery, making a kind of tapestry from this photograph of his face and I just had to capture it somehow. If only I could show you it now, his face and the photograph and my embroidery piece that I made from his face and the photograph. I mean, so beautiful, so tortured, so suffering. He looked up into a place above him and he was... pleading. For relief, for the end, to be let down from the cross, to be free from his commitment to the cross. And so beautiful. The depth of his shallow eyes. And the way his mouth slackly lay open.

VII

I had been standing staring at him on the cross for about half an hour. And that's when Douglas said, 'Do you know what's missing from my portrayal of Christ?'

And I said, 'Do tell.' His portrayal. Did you hear that?

And Douglas said, 'It's the crown of thorns. I've been thinking about it. Heavy hangs the crown and all that.'

And I said, 'Oh yes?'

And he said, 'Aye. I mean, without the crown... Crucifixion was common for hundreds of years. Without the crown and the insult of the "INRI", he could be—'

And I was like, 'Who? Who else is known for having been crucified?'

And he said, 'Offhand... Well... Spartacus.'

And I said, 'What?'

And he was like, 'I'm pretty sure at the end of the film *Spartacus* they all get crucified.'

And I said, 'So?'

And he said, 'And Brian, at the end of *The Life of Brian*. He's crucified.'

And I said, 'Are you joking? Are you pulling my leg?'

And he was like, 'It's just I've been thinking about the way I'm doing it.'

And I said, 'The way you're doing it? Doing this crucifix-ion. This one?'

And he said, 'Aye.'

And I said. 'Take a breather, get down. I've something I have to do.'

We had added this wee perch to take his body weight, something which I think is called a sedile that you sometimes see in Crucifixion images. So, he could actually get himself up on the cross and put his arms loosely in the bindings, which is how I painted sometimes. At other times I'd get up there, bind him tight and paint like that, and other times again he would slip his feet off the sedile and take the strain for as long as he could.

Anyway, for a wee while all I felt I could do was rearrange brushes and pots, every so often chucking one to the floor or across the room where a wee kitchen midden developed. Douglas took no notice, just happy to sit at the base of the cross, relieved to be able to slump and stretch forward, his shoulders towards his knees. Then I was walking rapidly to the door.

And I was like, 'I'll be back in a minute.'

Outside I just kind of stood against a wall and breathed, letting my shoulders slump forward too. Then I stood up straight and walked along to Kelvingrove Park, looking out a vaguely neglected flower bed at the entrance to the park at the corner of Gray Street and Parkgrove Terrace. My guess is there used to be a rose garden there. It wasn't there any more, but one bush had grown huge and wild, tucked away beside some trees. I returned to the studio loads more minutes more than one later, anyway, with a crown fashioned from rose-bush branches. I worked it into a dome shape as

I made my way back, and my fingertips were bleeding in a couple of places from thorn pricks. Douglas looked up and round at me. He had sat there the whole time.

And he was like, 'Right. I was thinking something a bit more, eh, benign. No so jaggy.'

And I was like, 'Oh? Like what?'

And he said, 'Well, some branches that you could just add the thorns into on the canvas.'

I stood there looking at him for a wee while. And he stood up slowly and turned and got back up on the cross. I got up on the ladder holding the fresh crown as gingerly as I could.

And I said, 'Are you ready?'

And he said, 'It's for the art.'

And I lowered the crown down on to his scalp, pushing it down gently, and he was swearing. I stopped.

And he said, 'No! Keep it going now if you're going to do it! Do it!'

I raised my hands and let them fall at the weight of themselves down on the crown and he was like, 'JESUS CHRIST!' and I was squealing too. The pain, and blood had started spotting his scalp and brow and the blood from my hands was starting to flow in little rivulets down my fingers and palms and was dripping off my wrists. And the overwhelming need I had was to laugh. Laugh! It was just so absurd. Douglas was wriggling his head, trying to get the blood from his forehead to run away from his eyes and by now he was screaming at the top of his voice, screaming, 'JESUS CHRIST, SUSAN ALISON! JESUS CHRIST! JESUS! CHRIST!'

I tried to prise my hands away from the crown, to get my hands free and lift it a little back off his head, but this was worse – the tiny hook-headed thorns tore at our skin even more than when I had been pushing down, and a stab shot along my arms and made my left arm quiver from fingertip to shoulder. A thorn had hit nerve. I've never got the feeling back in that finger since. Though, weird. Look at that. I seem to be able to feel something in the finger just now.

I had a hellish thought that I would just have to pull away as fast and violently as I could to free my hands so I could lift the crown off Douglas's head. Not a thought for sketch-books or photographs. My hands were in no condition. I couldn't take my eyes off my fingers and skin pinching and stretching on the tiny thorn heads. But I thought, if I look at his face, sear the image of his face and head into my brain and just don't look at my own hands for a second, I can get free. So I moved down a step of the ladder so that my hands were now over my head and my face was face to face with his face, and I peeled my hands, wrist to fingertips, over the dome of thorns, as quickly as I could, all the while staring directly into his eyes, his mouth (he was screaming and I saw the back of his throat), the blood flowing in rivers now down his nose, comically reddening the tip of his nose and dripping off. Laugh was still what I felt I needed to do.

Once I got my hands free, I admit I wasn't thinking about him much for a couple of minutes, just the burning tingling in my hands. I touched a finger here and there to my wounds, but it was almost like rubbing salt in them, like touching the wet painted surface that is clearly marked wet paint, because you have to.

And what was it all for? The painting still ended up a mess of overworked red and black abstract shapes and tones. As I moved away from it, thinking I had just then done enough, I realised how too-much I had actually done and wept. I wept. And I said, 'There's already too much going on.'

All this was going on and the world was going on around us. Did I mention yet that Douglas was in the Socialist Worker Party? Well, he was. Mibby I should have told you this sooner, though I'm not really sure that it explains anything about him. Except mibby that he and a couple of his Socialist Worker artist pals around this time – well, a couple of years earlier – had put together a kind of self-published book called *Artists in Revolt* (a titled adapted from a beat-writer anthology, *Writers in Revolt*), which featured photographs of their work and 'manifestos', mostly rambling gibberish about art as a revolutionary act. And, amazingly, the local press swallowed it, with the *Glasgow Herald* doing an article on the book with a photo of Douglas and his two pals looking suitably revolutionary, beards cut into Lenin goatees and all staring off into the sunny uplands of a socialist future. All very revolting.

What did I do about that? Well, every time he arrived at the studio I said, 'Did you hear? Thatcher's been deposed.' And because of the times we lived in then, and this would be Thatcherite times, if you can remember that far back, every single time he said, 'I knew it! It had to happen!'

And that's when I'd say, 'Actually, I'm only kidding.'

And he would be like, 'Are you sure?'

And I'd be like, 'Of course I'm sure. I make it up every time and you fall for it every time. I know when I'm making things up.'

And he was like, 'Well, after what she was saying yesterday, I wouldn't be surprised.'

What she was saying yesterday was anything that she said. He found it all offensive and reason enough to depose her. He kept saying to me, 'You have to read this really good book I have about it all.' Some Socialist Worker Party book, I doubt. Well, finally he was right, I guess. In the November of that year she was out on her ear. And of course, it just had to be the first time that when I got Douglas up out of bed when I had stopped off at his flat with a snowball on the way back from signing on and said 'Did you hear Thatcher's been sacked?', because he was too sleepy to be bothered he finally said, quite right too, given the circumstances, 'Aye, right.'

She, Thatcher, had looked like she was going to get out of the second-round vote scrape she was in.

And I said, 'No, really.' And then I said, 'I always hated her. I can remember her getting in, quoting Francis of Assisi. Nineteen seventy-nine. She was reacting to our winter of discontent. Rats in Glasgow. Where there is discord, let us bring harmony. Good God almighty. I'm glad her own side has crucified her – she deserves every last nail.'

And Douglas said, 'Aye. But.'

And I was like, 'But *what*?'

And he said, 'Well, if she's really over... I mean, best recruiting sergeant for socialism and that.'

And I said, 'It's still worth it.'

And he said, 'Suppose so.'

Man, he and his pals were drunk that night, and during this party Douglas predicted another party when he said, 'One day, in the future, when she cops hers, there's going to be a monster George Square Thatcher death party – like millions of people will spontaneously gather in George Square and

dance and sing and get minging. People are not for forgetting. It's a Brueghel waiting to happen.'

And I said, 'Brueghel? What's all this? What's going on?
What about you and your pals' revolution in art? What works
by you will be celebrated?'

And he said, 'Oh aye. I'll do a massive pish-filled grave-
stone for her and we'll put it up in George Square.'

But I'm kind of getting off the point because the point is
in that article with the picture of the Lenin beards and stares
off into the sunny uplands of the socialist Eden, right there in
the picture front and centre, of course, is the book, and at the
party that night I said to Douglas, 'How's the book?'

And he said, 'Selling brilliantly. Did you see us in the
paper?'

And for all I know all the money went to the cause, but all
I'm saying is it doesn't matter how revolutionary your art is:
if it doesn't sell, then no one knows about it.

It was getting towards Christmas and we were along
Dumbarton Road at this new restaurant called Two Fat
Ladies (it was at number eighty-eight, if that explains the
name for you) that had opened a few years before but, as I said
to Douglas, 'I don't know anyone who's been to it. Do you?'

And he said, 'Aye. Eh. I think so.'

It was a pretty fancy place and expensive, but I think
Douglas just wanted to have a blow-out, or, as it turned out,
he just knew more about how to get by than I did. As soon
as we had opened the door into the place one of the black-
trousers-and-shirt waiters waved at us from the back near the
kitchen. I thought he was just being the greeter guy but then
he goes and calls out, 'Cody!'

I think Douglas's eyes were adjusting to the light because he sort of peered at the guy for more than a couple of seconds without reacting, apart for this peering. Then he looked down at the toggles of this new cracker of a duffel coat he had on, which he was taking off. And I told him, 'That's a belter of a coat.'

And he was like, 'Aye? Aye, I'm worried this jacket has more personality than I have.'

After putting down this and lifting up that, the Two Fat Ladies guy started over to us and, as he approached, he was like, 'Cody!'

Douglas looked up and said, 'You all right, Alex?'

And this Alex said, 'Aye. Good. How are you doing?' Then, looking at the cuts and grazes on Douglas's head, he said, 'Jeez. What happened to you?'

Douglas looked at him for a wee while then smiled and said, 'It's nothing. Good to see you. I'm all right. This is Suse.'

And Alex said, 'Suse,' nodding at me. Then he turned back to Douglas and said, 'Been ages, eh?'

And Douglas said to me, 'Alex was on my foundation year.'

And Alex said, 'Aye. Cody the legend, eh? You know about him, I take it, Suse?'

I was taking my coat off and handing it to this Alex.

And Douglas said to Alex, 'Hold off.'

And Alex said, 'Eh? Aye. No problem. Do you lot have a booking? Tell you what. No bother whether you do or don't. I'll get you a table. Eh...' He looked around and said, 'This one here. Is that OK?'

And Douglas said, 'Fine.'

And I said, 'That's great. Thanks.'

And then Douglas said, 'I did actually book it.'

And Alex said, 'Aye? Great. Cool, Cody. No problems. Nice meeting you, Suse. I'll leave you with these,' and he handed us menus I hadn't even noticed he was carrying under his arm.

As we were sitting down I said, 'I didn't know you did a foundation year.'

And Douglas said, 'Doesn't everyone?'

The meal was good and I had two glasses of champagne that they sold by the glass and you didn't have to buy a full bottle. Douglas drank a bottle of white wine.

And I was like, 'Can you afford this stuff?' when I saw the price of the wine. He'd chosen the priciest bottle on the list.

And he was like, 'I'm making a bit of money now, and, anyway, I can get these things sorted out.'

I shrugged. The champagne was going to my head and I was starting to feel like I couldn't care less about paying for meals or how Douglas paid, though I was starting to kind of assume he was running up massive tabs all over town.

It was as we were leaving that the Alex guy came back over and started chatting again. And he said, 'Aye. Cody was the man. Off to do his conceptual stuff at the Art School, eh? And making money at it now. Magic.'

And Douglas said to Alex, 'You went to art school too.'

And Alex said, 'Fair enough. But I hudnae got the thing-ummy, you know, you meeting Joseph Beuys in nineteen seventy-six.'

And Douglas said, 'That was seventy-four. Still doing all right with the portraits? Getting commissions?'

And Alex said, indicating his waiter-wear, 'Well, as you can see, it's not quite making me money just yet.'

And then Douglas said, 'We're all in the same boat. Suse here works a couple of shifts in the Chip.'

And I said, 'No I don't. Why are you saying that? And you met Joseph Beuys?'

And Douglas said, 'Oh, I was under the impression...' Then he corrected himself and he said, 'I was thinking of someone else.'

And I said, 'And you met Joseph Beuys?'

And Douglas was like, 'My mother knew Ricky Demarco.'

And Alex said, 'Heh, Suse. You need to watch him.'

And I said, 'Sure,' while I was thinking about how lately I had been doing nothing but staring at him for hours on end and getting nowhere with my Crucifixion. That, and that next he'll be telling us that his uncle or something is Eduardo Paolozzi.

And Alex said, 'I see from the way things are going for you that you won't be wishing that you had stuck with the portraiture?'

And I was like, 'Portraiture?' Yet again I couldn't believe what I was hearing.

And Alex said, 'Oh, he was brilliant.'

And I said, 'Well!' But just at that minute I couldn't come up with anything else. I was speechless.

And Alex said to Douglas, 'Haven't you told her? Cody!'

And Douglas said, 'It hasn't come up.'

And Alex said, 'Kidding!'

And I said, 'What?'

And Douglas was stumbling over his words, 'Eh. I... I... Eh.'

And Alex said, 'God, if I had won the John Player Award I'd have told everyone.'

And I said, 'The John Player? The BP Award? The Portrait Gallery one?'

And Douglas was like, 'Eh, aye.'

And I said, 'I can't really believe what I'm hearing here.' I had kind of slumped back against the wall by the coat stand. And I said, 'How come I've never heard anything about this?'

And Douglas said, 'Eh...'

And Alex was like, 'Eh nothing. He won it before he even came to college for foundation. What age were you then, anyhow?'

And Douglas said, 'Eh. Um. Twenty? Nineteen, mibby.'

And Alex said, 'What year was that again?'

And Douglas was like, 'Nineteen seventy-nine?'

I was doing a quick calculation in my head and then I couldn't help but let out a sharp, 'Ha! You're older than you look.'

And Douglas said, 'I never said what age I was.'

I guess he was right, and although I knew he was a wee bit older than the rest of us I always thought it was just by a year or two. I suppose it's not that much more. Five years or so. But still. He did look younger than thirty now. But then I was thinking about how I had chosen him for my Crucifixion as he approached thirty and what had already fallen into place fell even more into place, if that's a thing that can be possible.

Alex was like, 'Told you, Suse. This messiah needs watching!'

And I was like, 'This what?' But before he had a chance to answer I said to Douglas, 'So what was this award-winning painting called?'

And Douglas said, 'It was a portrait. Portraits don't have painting names. They just are called the name of the person sitting for the portrait.'

I think I was shaking my head just looking at Douglas as he said something to Alex I didn't quite catch, then he turned to me and said, 'You head round to Tabak and get the drinks in and I'll settle up here. My treat.'

I mean, I know now what was going on – I probably even guessed back then that he was peeing into bags to pay for these meals. Scotland's shame!

As I left to walk out of Two Fat Ladies to go round to Tabak in Byres Road I saw Douglas and Alex talking and Douglas was holding his arms up like he was Atlas holding the world.

The truth is that by 1994 the world knew about Douglas, and his fame in Glasgow *had* grown to almost messianic proportions. It was something about him spending so much time in London now. People stared at him on the streets and in pubs as though he was a television celebrity. When we were out drinking you could watch young women circle and go past us three, four times, back and forth to the toilets. No one needs to pee that much. And though he never said anything to me about it, I knew he was sleeping with many of the women of the bohemian scene when he was back in Glasgow. And he was getting so drunk in the bars and restaurants of the city, where his pretty outrageous behaviour seemed to be excused by all and sundry, as long as the night ended with a pay-off of an example of one of his 'works'. It was appalling. Or let me be more specific. *I* was appalled. Frankly, he was acting like a little boy.

Though I was thinking of him this way, to art people he was like some sort of messiah – well, certainly some gallery owners thought of him this way. He was making packets of money for loads of them. And all this messiah jazz reminds me of this time we were on the Underground, heading out to the West End. There was this woman who was losing her rag with her wee girl, saying something like how both of them were tired because they had been shopping for hours and could she just not give her, the mother, a rest, and could she just not keep going on. The wee girl's whining and complaints became a sobbing and then piercing high-pitched crying and the mother was like, 'Oh for the love of God, will you just stop!' She was getting more and more flustered and the tension around us all was rising, like something was telling us that the mother was on the cusp of giving the kid a slap across the chops, and she said, 'Stop! STOP!', really abruptly and tugging at the wee girl's arm. And then she said, 'So help me, r—'

And that's when Douglas, who was standing next to me directly across from her and the kid, sort of leaned forward and down and reached out his hand and placed it on the mother's hand. And I was thinking, she's really going to go nuts at this, really going to turn on Douglas, and I was waiting for the screaming to begin, so I had shut my eyes for a second to somehow deal with the scene. But in the darkness all I heard was silence, or at least silence from them. I heard the *froofroofroofroofroofroo clank froofroo* of the wee train going along the tracks. I opened my eyes, and it was so weird but the mother was just looking up at Douglas smiling. He was so beautiful – angelic, sometimes. Then I saw he was smiling at her and he said, 'Love your child.'

And the mother said, 'What?'

And he said, 'She just needs a wee bit of love, your daughter. Love her.'

He took his hand off her hand and stood away from the mother and kid, turned as though he was about to continue his conversation with me as though nothing had happened. When I glanced at the mother and child again one last time before we were getting off at Partick, she, the wee girl, was happily, quietly sitting on her mother's lap, a little flushed, pink bundle of joy.

And I said to him, I said, 'Man, messing with a conniptious Glasgow mummy? You're mad. You should be dead now.'

And he said, 'She wasnae that nippy.'

And I said, 'Are you joking? Absolute miracle you got away with it. Feel like parting the Red Sea now?'

And he was like, 'Moses? I amn't.'

And I said, 'No, but the way that kid went pacified...'

And he was like, 'Listen, I know nothing about kids. I'm probably more likely to accidently kill any kid that comes within arm's length. Like Herod or something. Moses, I definitely amn't. Not the now, anyway. Mibby one day.'

One day I said to him, 'You know that way you light up reddy-pink when you put a torch up close to your fingers?'

And he says, 'Aye, what about it?'

And I said, 'The Grosvenor Cinema, over there,' (we were sitting in the Grosvenor Café when the Grosvenor Café was in the wee place across from the cinema, not in the cinema, like it is now, eating pizzas with a fried egg on top) 'they've got a klieg lamp and I'm sure it works.'

And Douglas was like, 'A what?'

And I said, 'Uch, you know, one of those cinema arc lights – you know, like a big spotlight that's used on movie sets to light everything up so's the camera captures everything. And then they shine them up into the sky at the première.'

And he said, 'Aye?' looking at me with a look on his face like he'd just said, 'Aw, aye?' Interested, but fearful too.

And I said, 'Well, I reckon they'd give us a loan of it for a wee while – God knows we spend enough time in their place. And I reckon it would look brilliant if we set it up behind the cross and lit you up from there. Do you reckon that you would light up see-through, pink and red and orange like your fingers do with a torch?'

And he says, 'Aye, I reckon I might.' He was warming to the idea and he said, 'The blood inside me, all lit up like that. Aye. You've got some ideas, Suse.'

And I said, 'You think it will work?'

And he said, 'Aye. Let's go and ask them right the now.'

I wanted to smash the Transfiguration and the Crucifixion and the Resurrection all together in one painting. He asked me what the Transfiguration was, and I told him it was when Jesus lit up on the mountain. He didn't seem to know about the Transfiguration. His knowledge of the Bible was Ballyhoo Zilch. He said he was never listening in RE.

Two days later we had it all set up and ready to go. We put the klieg up on a platform we had built so that it would be behind him at his back so that the dead centre of the light would be, from the front, at his solar plexus. The cross seemed to get in the way of what we were trying to achieve, so in the end he was on another platform tied in a kind of King Kong style between the wall and the upright sleeper, this to maintain the duress in his arms and take some of the weight. He was also hard up against the light for maximum effect. We had been holding our hands up to the light most of the morning, then our arms, and they had been lighting up nicely, pink-red, orange-red, orange-pink. It was brilliant.

And Douglas said, 'Fits in with my work.'

And I was like, 'How?'

And he says, 'Blood and pish, same stuff. Pish is blood filtered through the kidneys or something like that.'

And I said, 'What, you didn't even check this stuff before you started your work?'

And he said, 'Well, everyone knows about kidneys.'

And I said, 'Liver. How come with alkies it's their livers that go?'

And he said, 'Aye? Aye, right enough, never thought of that.'

So, anyway, he's up on the platform and I said, 'You ready?'

And he said, 'Aye! Totally into it.'

And I said again, 'You ready?'

And he said, 'Aye… wait… aye.'

I reached round and twiddled with the dials and flicked the switch at the back of the klieg.

The smell of burn hit before he screamed something that for the life of me sounded like, 'Yeeeeeeeeehaaaaaaa!' Like a cowboy, you know, and then he was like, 'JESUS, THAT'S HOT.'

I mean, we'd noticed the heat when we had our hands and arms up against the lamp, but I think because we were looking straight into it we had switched it on at the lowest setting. But when I switched it on for the Crucifixion it had flipped to full power somehow. The burning and pain hit his body and there was this kind of white-noise sound and Douglas was trying to move forward and up. He kind of looked like the Swan Song record label logo, the one that's similar to the Armory Show artist William Rimmer's drawing. But the bindings on his arms tugged him and made him fall and push back, and he was kind of stuck where he was, stuck in the bindings but also now like his skin and flesh was melting against the light. And because he pushed back he pushed the klieg hard up against the wall, which meant even if I hadn't been dunted clean off the platform on to the floor, I couldn't have got to the controls anyway. Then he lit up, like we thought he would, pink and orange and red. Absolute bloody pandemonium. And he was like, 'THE BINDINGS!' and screamed some more. And, then, the strangest thing, he was like, 'THE SUN SMELLS TOO LOUD!'

And I got up there to undo the bindings – not easy because he was writhing and they kept pulling tight, making the knots smaller and smaller. But finally (which makes it sound like a while, but it must have been about a couple of minutes of tugging and biting) I got him free. And then he kind of flew forward, like straight forward off the lamp – never seen anything like it: he kind of leaped off the platform into a freefall to the floor as this weird light filled the studio. Then he was on the floor and his back was all blood and black and burn and blister and wisps of smoke. And he was twitching. The twitching is what freaked me out the most. I was looking down at him from the platform. Always the twitching.

In the moments he was quiet on the floor after the twitching stopped I thought that I wished I'd had a camera ready for when he had turned pink, red, orange, and then I thought I shouldn't be thinking that, I should be thinking, 'Get to the phone box, you've got to phone an ambulance.'

When the ambulance people arrived Douglas was still face down on the floor, but by now he was talking and he just couldn't move. Not talking coherently, I mean. He was like, 'Burn, girl prom queen.' That kind of thing.

Then one of the ambulance paramedic's eyes started darting from the lamp (dead now – the thing had blown, which was why it got so hot), the canvas, the naked burnt man. I was looking at him looking around and before he could say anything I said, 'I was painting him. He's the model, I'm an artist.'

And the ambulance paramedic said, 'Right,' dressing yet another weeping, open blister. And then he said, 'I don't ask unless, you know, violence or something. Then I have to call the police – scene of a crime, you know? I thought this might be a, you know, slight domestic?'

And I said, 'Sure. Well, ask Douglas. This was more an accident, you know. Em… misadventure.'

And the paramedic said, 'I wouldnae use that term, love. That makes people think of "death by misadventure". Yer man here, he's going to be sore, all right, for months yet, probably, but he'll make it. After a wee while in the burns unit.'

And I said, 'Well, OK. Let's call it a technical hitch.'

VIII

Christmas 1994 came and all over there were Christmas lights and Christmas trees and the Christmas song (there are, of course, many Christmas songs, but to me they all sound the same, and Christmas trees are, by definition, all at least similar, if not identical, and let's face it, once you've seen one fairy light you've seen them all) and we thought about the baby Jesus, the babe in a manger, the birth of the Saviour, instead of thinking about torturing the man upon the cross. I don't know why, but now, when I think of Glasgow, I think of Christmas.

I remember Douglas said, 'Do you know that all Renaissance baby Jesuses are really ugly wee old men?'

And I said, 'Why?'

And he said, 'Uch, because they were all trying to paint the soul of a god inside a man, inside the baby. Because he had been a god, Jesus, always been part of God, the Trinity, and now he was a wee baby. But there was also God inside the man inside the child.'

And I said, 'What do you mean? He was a baby. Born then. Wasn't that when Jesus started?'

And he said, 'No. No. You have to know that after Jesus was born a man there had to have always been a Jesus, and a

Trinity for ever, you know, with God the Father and that. And the Holy Ghost.'

And I said, 'Spirit.'

And he said, 'Aye. Always. In heaven, or wherever they come from.'

And I said, 'God lives in heaven?'

And he said, 'Aye. Where else?'

And I said, 'Well, at the start of the Bible he's, well, nowhere. Isn't he? The Void. Before he makes heaven and earth.'

And he was like, 'Aw aye. You're right. I suppose he made heaven to live in.'

And I said, 'Why? Why didn't he live on earth? I mean like, wasn't he on earth in the Garden of Eden, talking to Adam and Eve?'

And he said, 'I think he was talking to them from heaven. From on high, you know?'

And I said, 'Man. Must have had a loud voice!'

And Douglas was like, 'Aw, what? God? Aw aye. Booming. Big, booming… voicemonger, God. Have you no read the Bible?'

And I said, 'My mithair… My mother preferred to read it to me.'

And he said, 'Aye. Naw, me neither. But you must have heard of him. God. He's big. Big character in the story, know? Top man. Big cheese, the high heid yin, the centre of the whole plot, the whole shebang. The big kahuna. The big apple.'

And I said, 'The Big Apple? That's New York, you numpty.'

In 1995 Douglas moved to New York on a semi-permanent basis, though he still spent time in London and Glasgow as well. Quite touchingly, he told me the only thing he would come back to Glasgow for with any frequency would be to model for me. And he said, 'It's meant something to me, Susan Alison. I don't think you realise.'

I think he was right. I hadn't thought it had meant much to him. But, then, why did he keep on turning up for the gig? On the other hand, what the realist inside me had realised was that he was only saying this about coming back from New York because somewhere deep inside he suspected I was on the cusp of giving up on the Crucifixion. He suspected I was getting to the end of the line, that I couldn't stand the failure of it all any more. I suspect his suspicions were not unfounded. He could see the tears well up in my eyes as we reached the end of sessions and I added this and redid that and painted over the other, the paint pasted on thicker and thicker, it all going the same abstract way as before and me seemingly unable to stop myself. Was I really going to go on doing this to myself, and to him? It was self-lacerating. I was like a self-flagellant.

They knew it was coming, the women of the arts scene. And it was like they had gone into mourning. Well, I tell you, when they heard, Isobel and Amanda and Marion and Anna, Jenny and Rona and Mairi, Katrina and Maureen and Alison and Bernice, Katy and Frances and Maria, Sharleen and Kate and Nikki and Shonagh and all of them, when they heard he was leaving... pandemonium. You have to understand, he was just so very beautiful – more beautiful than Jamie, the guy they let come here to cut my hair, and God, is *he* beautiful. And I'll tell you an open secret from them last few years, he had slept with well over half of them. He would be together with one or other of them for a couple of days, then there would be a wee pause in festivities for a few months and then another of them would be his partner for a wee while, then back he would go to one of them, then on to another... It was all so accepted because everyone knew how it would run, and each of them, Amanda and Marion and Rona, Jenny and Mairi and Anna and Katrina and Bernice and Alison and Maureen and Sharleen and Katy and Maria and Frances, Kate, Nikki and Isobel and all of them knew the score. It, *he*, Douglas, was like a ritual to be performed, that they performed. Their time in the presence of Douglas, their communion with him. Like the brides of Christ nuns, they somehow wedded Art by sleeping with Douglas for short periods of time. Until, that is, they found some more permanent partner or got married for real.

It probably was time for him to move on for real, and perhaps secretly – a secret I kept even from myself – I was hoping that him going would make me forget about the Crucifixion, make me give up on it, the whole sorry series of messes. On the evening before the last evening before he flew to New York we went for a nice meal at the Chip, with his usual palaver of peeing in a bag for the bill. Would you believe by this stage, though he had actually offered to pay for once, the people there said they'd prefer the 'artwork', that it was worth more to them.

And I said, 'What are you going to title this one?'

And he said, 'Dunno. *The Last Supper*?' And then he saw I was about to cry, I think, and said, 'I'll call it *Untitled*. We all know what it is, after all.'

And I said, 'I certainly do.'

And he was like, 'Aye? What do you mean?

And I said, 'Nothing.'

He sat back and took his glass of wine and raised it to me, but I didn't move to respond. I was actually too raging to 'cheers'. As he left me that night we hugged a last time and he lifted me up off the ground and kissed my forehead. And he said, 'May nothing but happiness come through your door. Remember, Suse, there's no medicine for regret.'

Then... and I was just on the cusp of saying 'then suddenly', but it couldn't have been 'suddenly' at the time, can it, because what I'm saying is that then it had been days, then weeks, then months that he had been away in New York. These are the facts. The difficult truth, as they say. And the only truth that mattered to me was that, really, I was as miserable as sin and I missed him. I missed Douglas. For a while. Then that feeling went away. It's not as if I've ever been obsessed with the guy. I'm not now, and I wasn't then.

Then the horror began, them coming to me, usually alone, one time two of them, and the conversation would always start off normal, a bit of chit-chat – you know, 'How are you?' and 'How are you and how's work coming along?' and 'What are you working on now?' and 'Who got this or that commission or this or that job?' And then the same thing every time. About fifteen minutes in Isobel or Amanda or Anna, Jenny, Rona or Katrina or Alison or Katy and Frances or Kate or Shonagh would kind of, well, burst into tears. Then for a while it was all a wee bit individual. All of them were unhappy about the same thing, Douglas being in New York, but all of them were unhappy about it in slightly different ways. How they had been *so* in love with him but just hadn't realised it, how they couldn't love anyone else, how he had been awful to them but that was just them misunderstanding him, how he had misunderstood them, how they wished they had settled down with him, married him, had his babies, how they felt they were nothing without him, how they didn't know how to love him, how he didn't know how to love them. Him him him. Them them them. Love love love love love. God almighty!

And always the last stuff, after the teas and the hankies, the last pleading, 'Do you know when he's going to be over?', 'Is he coming back, for a wee while or for good?', 'What are his plans?'

We were like some big weird family, and it was almost... well, it was like it wasn't like a sexual thing, what with the accumulation, it wasn't like some dream husband was gone, but like... like we were all his sisters and he was the beloved older brother, killed in the war or something like that. And they were so bitter, sometimes, like he had abandoned us. Not them individually, but *us*. Am I explaining this right? Am I making it sound weird? Because, believe me, it was weird. Sometimes families just feel like a bitterness centrifuge or something with hate and love going round at a million miles an hour and it all causing suddenly strong, suddenly weak forces, a rollercoaster going strong, weak, strong, weak. Relative hysteria, you know?

I don't know. What was love to him, anyway, that kind of love? The kind of love that makes you feel those forces? I mean, God is love, isn't it? That's a quote from the philosopher, 'the Evangelist'. 1 John, chapter 4, verse 8. See, I can do that when I want to, quote chapter and verse. Well, I can sometimes, for favourite quotes. But that's not the kind of love we are talking here, is it? Not really. It was the love of wanting to be near the desired one, to penetrate and be penetrated by, in the physical and spiritual and sensual and sexual way. To love. To be loved. To reach to somewhere else, to be raised high by this love, the ecstasy. Which is to say the overwhelming joy but also the mystical experience. And to do that with and because of another human being. Come on. Douglas in his fifteen or forty-eight or seventy hours with one of them before he said, 'You know this has been great...'

I don't think so. I don't think he needed that love. He was being adored too much and too often to bother with that kind of love, the love that is less 'God is love' and more 'Love is God'. That love I don't think he needed at all.

In some way, mibby, he loved like Jesus loved, which is to say, well, not individually. Unless God is an individual, though Jesus himself sort of puts paid to that idea by being God too, part of the Trinity. Because, think about it, when it comes down to it, in the Gospels, Jesus seems to me to love God and humanity and that's it. I mean, who did he love other than that? His apostles and disciples? Even the blessed mother isn't shown receiving any act of kindness or consideration or sonly devotion, is she? I am genuinely asking, as I'm trying to remember an instance. Does he do a miracle one time at her request? Mibby so. But genuine, authentic love for his mother? She really is just there to give birth to him and raise him (although even this seems to only be partially), then to weep at the foot of his Crucifixion at the end. Seems a bit of a raw deal, really. But he doesn't seem to me to love like a son, and he doesn't love like a lover, nor a husband, and he of course does not love like a father. But, then, I guess we have God the Father to fulfil that role. All just seems a bit remiss somehow. He had no kids, so's he's no father, he never married, so's he's no husband, never had a lover, so's he is no lover's lover. I mean, mibby he wasn't even a son – a son of Mary, I mean. Thinking about it, was Jesus placed inside Mary by God...? I mean, was it *her* ovum? If it was, did God, then, *impregnate* Mary? That sounds a wee bit too Greek gods and nymphs, doesn't it? Oh, I'm giving myself a headache.

So mibby it was that Douglas loved the women artists and musicians and some civilians (who knows who they all might have been). He loved to be the centre of attention of the bohemians, and he'd to spread his love around, mibby? But then, that brings us back to if it's like that then is that really love? I mean, *really* love? Mibby he loved limitlessly. I mean, mibby he loved us all, loved everyone. Or mibby he loved no one. Or no one but himself?

Yes, mibby he loved no one but himself. But the truth is I was sorely missing him, too. It's difficult to even speak of the utter despair I was feeling at the progress of my Crucifixion. Just nothing was going anywhere and everything was going nowhere and, if anything, everything was regressing, sinking, failing. I couldn't think what to do, in my art or in my life, so I did what I always do in these instances. I went back to the island to see my mithair. She was in an interesting phase in her life, in her belief system. Very interesting. Almost straight away she said to me, 'Have you heard about the aliens, Susan Alison?'

And I said, 'What, incomers? Foreigners? Mainlanders?'

And she said, 'No. From outer space.'

Did I think she was joking? I said, 'Go on.'

And she said. 'Still, it will all be all right.'

And I said, 'Oh yes?'

And she said, 'Aye, well, the angels.'

And I was like, 'Well, of course. Angels versus aliens. No contest.'

And my mithair said, 'They look over us, don't they, Susan Alison?'

And I said, 'Of course. They look over you, Mummy.'

And she said, 'And you, Susan Alison, isn't that right?'

And I said, 'Oh, yes, Mummy. The angels, of course. My angel is on my shoulder.'

And she was like, 'What? What are you talking about, Susan Alison? An angel's too heavy to be on your shoulder. Dear Lord, Susan Alison.'

And I said, 'Of course, I meant...'

And she was like, 'Oh, you meant, you meant, you always mean, don't you?'

And I said, 'I... My guardian...'

And she said, 'Yes. Aye.'

It was a conversation to almost take the breath out of you. I mean, I always knew she believed in this and that and the next thing and it never bothered her that all these things seemed mutually defeating, like if you believe in God you are simply not supposed to believe in fairies and trolls, and if you believe in aliens, doesn't that make it harder somehow to believe in God, because, you know Patrick's friend Simon's comment about whose god would God then be, ours or the aliens'?

And I said, 'Mummy, are you feeling all right?'

And she said, 'I am. What do you mean?'

And I said, 'Well, you just seem a wee bit flushed, that's all.'

And she said, 'Did you just hear what I was saying to you, Susan Alison?'

And I said, 'Yes, Mummy, but —'

And she said, 'Well, if you had been hearing rumours about spaceships over Glasgow then maybe you would understand. But they're not in Glasgow, they're up here in the islands.'

And I said, 'Who told you? Who's telling you this stuff?'

And she said, 'Everyone is talking.'

And I said, 'Everyone? Are you sure?'

And she said, 'Oh, you sound like your faither!'

And I said, 'Well, if he's saying it's unlikely to be true then I would want to be like my faither.'

And she said, 'Are you accusing me of being a liar?'

And I said, 'No. No, of course—'

And she was like, 'Because I have never told a lie in my entire life.'

And I was like, 'Well, it just seems a wee bit far-fetched.'

And she was like, 'Far-fetched? Me never telling a lie or the aliens?'

And I said, 'Well, em, both, of course.'

And she said, 'Honestly, Susan Alison... I don't... I know you are, but what am I? I'm a godly woman.'

And I was about to say to her about belief and believing contrary stuff, but instead I said, 'Oh yes, Mummy, you are the most godly woman I know.' Though, really, I couldn't give a toffee if she was or wasn't or whether she believed me or not.

Believe it or not, his soul was what some of them said they missed. Some of them actually said that about him, Douglas. That they missed 'being in the presence of such a soul'. Jesus Christ! They really did make me want to puke.

There was this time we, Douglas and me, realised we knew this guy, both of us. He was like, 'You know, there was this guy at my school, Xander MacDonald.'

And I was like, 'Alexander MacDonald? I knew a Xander MacDonald at my primary school.'

And he was like, 'Just primary school?'

And I was like, 'After that he went to secondary school in Glasgow.'

And he was like, 'Hutchie? Like me?'

And you'll be like, 'Hutchie? You haven't mentioned this.' But, look, I'm not going to go into every revelation I ever had about Douglas. He went to Hutchie on a scholarship. I mean, is it that surprising? Hutchie, in case you don't know your Glasgow stuff, is the private school – they say independent school – Hutchesons' Grammar School on the south side of Glasgow. Till his O levels. It was one of the big reasons he knew bugger all about his own religion, because it's not a Catholic school.

And I was like, 'I know the guy. Knew him. He was a bit of a wee bully.'

And Douglas was like, 'Really? I thought he was OK.'

And I said, 'Not the way I remember him. Mibby two different guys with the same name?'

And he said, 'You think?'

And I said, 'It happens.'

And he said, 'And both called Xander for Alexander?'

And I said, 'It happens. On the islands, at least, there's always fourteen of every name.'

And he said, 'What was your guy like?'

And I was like, 'Thick neck, stocky rugby nut.'

And Douglas was like, 'Aye? That's my guy too.'

And I said, 'Yes, well, I didn't think much of him.'

And he said, 'I suppose… I mean, he could be a wee bit…'

And I said, 'He certainly could.'

And Douglas said, 'Mibby. I mibby got him wrong.'

And I was like, 'The biggest arse that ever came off the arsehole production line, pal.'

And Douglas was like, 'Really? Aw, come on.'

And I said, 'You think?'

And he said, 'He was just this meathead. He meant no harm, not by secondary, anyway.'

131

And I was like, 'Yes?'

And he was like, 'Obviously not in your book.' The point being that I was thinking about this just recently, in one of my wee dwams that I get to have a fair few of these days, and it led me back to this realisation that I had met Douglas when we were both at the Art School and that we had remembered and spoken about it in the days I was painting him. I was sitting in the library. He came up behind me, Douglas, and whispered in my ear, 'One of these days I'm going to burn this place to the ground.'

And I turned and looked up at him and said, 'Oh yes? Why?'

And he said, 'Dunno. A phone call. Someone will tell me to do it.'

And I said, 'What did you dial? Revenge?'

And he said, 'All shall suffer. Then they'll know who I am.'

When I reminded him of this he said, 'Aye? Aye, I was always saying stuff like that to complete strangers. Did you hate me? Did you think I was weird?'

And I said, 'You overestimate… or, rather, underestimate how much all you Art School boys are apt to say weird things out of the blue.'

And he said, 'Aye? Aye, I suppose.'

The Mackintosh building actually burning down, and burning down twice, reminded me. Mibby the soul of him did it. Tell *that* to the ladies of this canyon.

IX

We were both going to stay with a friend of mine in a place
just north of Porto in Portugal in the late summer of 1996 –
if I remember correctly in the August. But first, in Lisbon, we
stopped off to see this gallery owner *slash* collector who had
just bought a few of his works. I don't know whether Douglas
wanted to thank him or something, I don't even know how
he knew the collector wanted to see him. But the three pieces
having sold for six figures up, I could see why thanks could
be in order. We got there and this wee guy and this pal of his
who was also wee, the two of them making me feel average
height and making Douglas look like a giant, got us glasses of
Portuguese wine and showed us into the gallery space where
the works were. We stood around for a wee while, sort of
making small talk mainly, with gestures, as the Portuguesers
only had a smattering of English and Douglas and me had
no Portuguese at all. Then Douglas was sort of gesturing
that he wanted to see something, some paperwork that the
art should travel with and the Portuguesers obliged and he
was looking at this paperwork and nodding. Then we were
sort of looking at other pieces in the gallery for a minute or
so and drifting away from the wee guys when Douglas sort of

pulled me off to the side and said in a stage whisper, 'What am I going to do? They're no my works. Someone has been ripped off. I mean, I'm looking at the authentication paperwork here and it's my name on it, my signature. But these are no my work. What should I do? Should I tell them?'

And I was like, 'Of course you need to tell them – how much money have they just spent?'

And he was like, 'Aye? Aye, of course. I need to?'

And I said, 'Yes. Don't you think they need to know?'

And he was like, 'Jeez. Someone is ripping me off? Why?'

And I said, 'Are you looking for an answer other than "To make money"?'

And he said, 'Yes, but why me? I knew it. Travel is dangerous.' Then he thought and then he said, 'I suppose my prices are getting good.'

And I said, 'And mibby someone thought the art would be easy to make.'

And he said, 'What do you mean by that? Those arenae even that well done. I suppose that's what you mean. Really the forgery of the signature is the—'

And I said, 'They're starting to wonder what we're rabbiting about.'

And he said, 'Heh, mibby it's a prank, an art prank. Banksy or something. That would be cool.'

And I said, 'Are you going to tell them?'

And he said, 'Aye. I better tell them. Wait. What's this going to do to my prices?'

And I was like, 'Eh?'

And he said, 'This could sink my prices.'

And I said, 'I think you still have a duty.'

And he said, 'Aye? Aye, you're right. Of course.'

Anyway, so happens the other wee guy with the gallery owner was one of Lisbon's top art critics and after the shock of the telling and then the unexpected delight came the newspaper story and the international sensation and all that, and of course Douglas's prices went up and people also flocked to see forgeries of bags of urine, not even that well done. That, it seems, is the way the art market works. It's the way of the world.

After this we had to head west out of town to see the *Estádio Nacional*, because this was where the Lisbon Lions, the Celtic team of legend, had won the nineteen sixty-seven European Cup, and Douglas wanted to see it. And I was like, '*Football?* What about Luis Buñuel?'

And he was like, 'Oh, my betrayal of Luis Buñuel? *Big* deal. It's not just football. The Lisbon Lions. More like religion.'

And I was like, 'And I have to come along because...?'

And he goes, 'To pal along with me and that, that's all. Come on. Come and see something *real* in the world.'

Real. Huh. Later, settled on the train on our way to see the friend north of Porto, I remember we were talking about authenticity certificates like the one that had been faked for the forgeries and about the way of the world and about the word 'authentic' again and the authentic and fake word of God and about the Bible and I said to Douglas, 'Well, it just seems a bit, you know, remiss of... God.'

And he said, 'What are you talking about?'

And I said, 'You know, remiss of God to send down his messenger, his *son*, for God's sake, his *only son* and, well...'

And he said, 'I'm not getting you.'

And I said, 'Look at it this way. Great philosophers, right? Well, they did philosophy, and when did that really take off so we can know about it now, these days? When they could actually write something down, notate their thoughts so we can know them and judge if they were any good.'

And he said, 'Well, I suppose the disciples and apostles and other people wrote down what Jesus said, his teachings.'

And I said, 'Yes, but if you were God and you were thinking, I want my message of love or whatever to be taken to earth, the world, wouldn't you send a great writer who would write this good book, this ultimate book of meaning, so that it could be spread among the people of the world? Wouldn't that be the best way? If you were going to make him a man with a man's lifetime on earth and you wanted the message to live on and on? I mean, and this was a literate time. Plato had written books. The library at Alexandria was full of books before the time Jesus was alive. Don't you think it was just a teeny weeny wee bit remiss of God to send a man into an illiterate world of fishermen in Galilee if he wanted the story to have any credibility or easy chance of being communicated around the world?'

And he said, 'Well, it seems to have worked out OK for them.'

And I said, 'Yes, but don't you think, looked at this way, it's not just remiss, it's perverse, like mibby God was thinking, "Hmmm... mibby this message of mine, love and conquered sin and all that, mibby it's a bit, oh, I don't know, crap?"'

And he said, 'Well, nice to know the mind of God.'

And I said, 'We know, supposedly, the actions of God. He's up there, thinks, "Hmm, sending the only son to earth with a huge message... I'll make him the illiterate son of a carpenter," because Jesus would have been illiterate, too, in this society, and Jesus was a carpenter too, right, till he was thirty.

Then he starts his ministry. So, he's got the message of God *from* God, his Heavenly Father. And that's got to be persuasive, right? It's the all-powerful God's message. So does Jesus go to the highest authority he can in the world? No, he starts preaching to nobodies in Galilee. It just makes no sense.'

And Douglas said, 'Think you're being a bit hard on the man. He was just who he was. You're working the joke by supposing this big, can-do-anything God guy. Mibby it's not like that.'

And I said, 'Listen, if God isn't the big, can-do-anything guy then he's not God. The story demands that.'

And he said, 'But you've said you don't believe any of this stuff, anyway. That it's not necessary to.'

And I said, 'I don't. That's not the point. I would appreciate it if the story made any sense at all. That's all I'm saying. Like look at all the time spent establishing this sparkling genealogy for Jesus, King David and all that, and back to Adam, the first man.'

And he said, 'Aye? So?'

And I was like, 'Well, how does it matter who he was the son of among the tribes of Israel if he was actually the son of *God*?'

And he was like, 'Well…'

And I was like, 'And anyway, his earthly father, or whatever, foster father or adoptive father, Joseph… he just disappears in the story, presumed dead at the end because Jesus says one of the disciples is to look after the blessed mother. That's a real measure of bad fiction, that is, carelessness with the minor characters.'

And he was like, 'Well… Bad. That's big. A big claim. I'll be the judge of that.'

And I was like, 'Well nothing. And family values being Christian values? You know how much Jesus says about marriage being a good thing in the Gospels? Nothing. Zilch. Do you know how often he's described visiting his blessed mother in between being born of her and laid in her arms at the end? Zilch!'

And he said, 'Naw. Look. Stories don't have to have meaning the way you're saying for them to mean things to people. And anyway, it's the easiest trap to fall into, explaining faith with logic and rationalisations.'

And I said, 'What? Have you not heard of exegesis? That's hundreds of thousands of people taking millions of hours to explain exactly what it's all about to billions of people. Worshippers. Whatever you want to call them.'

And he said, 'Sometimes I just think it's history. Naw? Just that. Like, it just so happens, at the approximate changeover from people wanting the gods to them having a desire for monotheism, one true God and all that, that a man in Galilee got nailed up on a cross, when all he had done was say something like "love one another"—'

And I said, 'And claimed to be their god.'

And he said, 'Aye, and that as well... In fact, wasn't he saying he was the god of everyone, not just of the Jews? Wasn't that the real frightener for everyone? Anyway, I'm saying the two things, man on cross, we want God in recognisable form, means man on cross becomes God. It was just a kind of year zero thing. Right place, right time. Do you see what I'm saying?'

And I said, 'I hear what you are saying. And all that religion and artefacts of religion and art of religion and explanation of the religion and explanation of the art of the religion... it's all...'

And he said, 'OK. Fair enough. But where have you got yourself to? God's not the greatest at PR? Look, the words of Christ, the ones he either did or did not say, that was all OK. But it's the story. Naw? It's what happened to him that is the real message. I mean, you're not painting him at the Sermon on the Mount, are you? I mean, people do. But it's the Crucifixion. That's the real meat. Naw?'

And I said, 'Of course. Of course. But what does it mean?'

And he said, 'Aye. Well. That's still, and always has been, where you've got me. An idiot god and a dope for a son. I'm imagining Jesus just toppled right off the cross in a comedy oops moment where no one had noticed the cross-beam wasn't nailed to the upright quite as fast-holding as everyone thought. I've got the family and friends making Oooh! Ouch! faces and the centurions pissing themselves laughing.'

And I said. 'Yes… yes.'

And he said, 'Is this going to be it? Are you thinking of painting it that way now? *The Crucifixion Carnival of Comedy*, you can call it. That might get you the column inches.'

And I said, 'Do you think that's what this's about?'

And he said, 'Among other things, it should be. Don't you learn anything from me?'

And I said, 'From you?'

And he said, 'Well, I am successful.'

And I was like, 'And I'm not?'

And he was like, 'I didn't say that.'

And I said, 'But it's what you meant.'

And he said, 'All I'm saying is you can get more art out there more of the time and make more money from it. What's so wrong with the plan?'

And I said, 'Your plan? Let me count the ways.'

And he said, 'Suit yourself, Susan Alison. You always do.'

And I said, 'And what's that supposed to mean?'

And he said, 'I think we already decided we don't know what any of this means, or, if we could admit it, we know it doesn't mean anything at all.'

And I was like, 'Nothing at all?'

And he said, 'God, Susan Alison, God is just a child's toy, you know what I mean?'

I didn't, but I didn't ask him what he meant either.

But it wasn't nothing means anything for me then. It was in 1996 that I received what I have to admit was my most life-changing and career-enhancing opportunity and biggest commission to date, when I was asked to create a triptych altarpiece for the third altar in St Paul's Cathedral in London. I could barely believe that the Church commissioners were willing to take a chance on me when, even though some of my figurative work was in circulation and had been critically lauded, my Crucifixions had all ended in abject and abstract failure.

But they wanted to talk to me, so I went along on a Tuesday to meet them, three of them. I don't know whether I was expecting a bunch of bishops or something, three middle-aged to elderly – grey haired at least – men dressed in bishops' get-up, full purple cloaks and wee hats, birettas or mitres, are they called? Us all sitting around, drinking tea and eating cake, like some Luis Buñuel scene. I was right about the grey-haired men aspect, wrong on the clothes. They were all dressed in sober, vaguely out-of-date suits, two charcoal and one relatively flamboyant blue pinstripe. More like a bunch of lawyers than Church people.

After they introduced themselves, names I instantly forgot, roles in St Paul's I had no framework to understand the hierarchy of, one of the charcoals said, 'We're very excited about your work forming part of the fabric of the old girl.' Honestly. 'The old girl.' It was hard not to laugh.

And pinstripes said, 'Yes. Absolutely.'

And the second charcoal goes, 'We've been recommended your work by something of an art insider.'

And I said, 'Oh? Who?'

And the second charcoal looks at the other two and hesitates, though the other two are looking at me with kind of fixed grins and not back at charcoal two. And he said, 'Well, I'm not sure I can really...'

And I said, just to kind of end the misery and move along, 'Oh I'm sure I don't have to know. I'm just really happy that I've come to your notice. And you want me to create new work, you said...' They were looking disconcertingly blank, and I said, '...in your letter. It's so exciting.' I winced, thinking that I must have sounded like an eager teenage granddaughter to them.

And pinstripes said, 'Yes. Absolutely.'

I looked at him for a moment, his fixed grin, feeling repetition of these words was going to be his whole contribution to the conversation.

Second charcoal said, 'We've been shown some photographs of the sort of things you've been working on.'

And I was like, 'Eh? I mean, oh? I mean, I'm not sure how you might have—'

And first charcoal said, 'Perhaps your work is more well known than you think.'

And I said, 'Yes. Well. Mibby.'

And charcoal two said, 'Oh, we think so. Your Crucifixion series.'

And I was like, 'Yes. My Crucifixion series? You know about them?'

And charcoal one said, 'Oh yes. Very much so.'

And pinstripes said, 'Yes. Absolutely.'

And charcoal one parroted, 'Yes, absolutely.'

And I was like, 'OK. But whoever you lot are getting this stuff from, you must know that none of those paintings have ever really worked out the way I wanted them to.'

And pinstripes said, 'Oh?' and I was thinking, Jesus, he does have another response, then. Also, his grin was gone, replaced with a look of... what? Perplexed curiosity?

Both the charcoals were saying something along the lines of, 'Oh, I'm sure not.'

And I was like, 'Really. I mean, I've never sold any of them. In fact, I've often thought of destroying most, well, all of them. Some of them definitely got painted over with other versions of them.'

And charcoal two said, 'Really? How fascinating!'

And charcoal one said, 'That's not the way things look to us. The descriptions we've heard and the photographs we've seen. We're very excited.'

And I was like, 'Yes, but you can't have... I mean, I don't know which you've seen or the quality of the photographs, wherever they came from... but, mibby you could... I mean, I wonder if you could see something of the original intention in them in... photographs. But, really, I can't see how you could have seen in them...'

And pinstripes, who had suddenly come to life like Lazarus, was like, 'Oh you're so wrong, Miss MacLeod.'

And I was like, 'Oh? OK.'

And he said, 'We love your work. To be honest, we wouldn't be here today unless we had been completely bowled over by the Crucifixion series.'

And I was like, 'Crucifixion series? What Crucifixion series? You keep— Really, I never intended a series, and the paintings aren't called that. They've never even been shown, and I thought only me and the model—'

And pinstripes – he actually seemed the one in charge – said, 'Oh, there's a model! How wonderful!' and the charcoals were nodding dogs all over that.

And I was like, 'Are you absolutely sure you know what paintings you've been shown? You don't happen to have the photographs, do you?'

Pinstripes and second charcoal both looked to first charcoal, so I guess he was the man on the photographs front. And I said, 'The photographs?' to him.

And he said, 'I think I can probably get my hands on them.'

We had been talking standing up – the conversation had kind of taken off before we'd got the chance to sit in these really plush chairs that looked as though they had been placed in preparation for our meeting – in this office kind of room, though more like a sitting room than a place with photocopiers and that kind of thing in it. Finally, three of us sat down in the chairs and second charcoal disappeared to get the photographs. During a weird sort of silence that crept out over a couple of minutes, which pinstripes finally broke by offering tea that I accepted but did not then ever receive, I thought about how the hell they could possibly have got photographs of the paintings. I mean, I had taken a few myself, but only because I tended by 1996 to take photos of works in progress, especially works in progress I had every intention of dumping. But who had I given these photos to ever? No one I could remember. Douglas? And then there were a couple of times in the last few years where journalists wanted a photo of me in front of one of my works in the studio. There had been a few of these articles, including one article about the peculiarity of the studio itself, in some Sunday supplement. Had the failed Crucifixion paintings ever been in the background? I'm sure if I had noticed they might be I'd have moved them out of the way.

When charcoal two got back he showed me three black and white bad photocopies of the pictures of the Crucifixion that had ended up as the blue and black moonscape mush, the red and black drippy seascape and the yellow and black swirly nothing. I stared down at them and couldn't seem to take my eyes off them as the men, commissioners, whoever, talked around me. They were saying something about *spiritual feeling*, I think.

And pinstripes said, 'Oh yes. Absolutely. The depth of feeling.'

And charcoal one said, 'Yes, I know what you mean. I could look into them – not at them, mind – *into* them all day. See the way a sine wave seems to run through this one?'

And charcoal two said, 'Yes, yes, yes. I totally agree. Totally. Spiritual.'

And pinstripes said, 'Like looking into a soul. A sometimes serene, a sometimes tortured soul.'

And I said, 'And these are the... the kind of paintings you want in this... commission? This's what you want in the cathedral? Abstracts?'

And pinstripes said, 'Oh yes. Absolutely. I thought we had mentioned...' he looked at one of the others, then the other other, and he said, 'in the letter... that it was the Crucifixion series, a continuation of that, that we were... looking for. Did we?'

And I was like... well, speechless for a while, actually.

They said things like, 'It'll be so miraculous... heavenly... contemplative...'

And I said, 'And these are the kind of paintings you want in this commission? This is what you want in the cathedral. Abstracts.'

And pinstripes said, 'Yes! Absolutely!' He was so happy.

And for a wee while I sat there, staring, smiling – dare I say it? – abstractly, hearing only babble from them talking between themselves until, fading back in, coming back from fuzzy to clear, I was hearing this sort of well-rehearsed Socratic dialogue between them, running something like this, with pinstripes saying, 'Oh, now, really, in what way can God have volume? In what way can he be viewed as being contained in any organic or inorganic entity?'

And charcoal one said, 'God is not an abstract concept.'

And pinstripes said, 'Of course God is. God is everywhere and always, outside space and time—'

And charcoal two said, 'Oh, come on.'

And charcoal one said, 'You make Him sound as though he is nowhere at no time!'

And pinstripes said, 'How can you *possibly* get that from "everywhere and always"? God is indivisible, in everything—'

And charcoal two said, 'In everything or everything itself? There's a difference.'

And pinstripes said, 'Look, take the case of Jesus—'

And charcoal two said, 'I cannot believe you are back on this "God is like mathematics more than He's like a man" thing *again.*'

And pinstripes said, 'God *is* more like mathematics than a man! Or more like time. Of course He is.'

And charcoal two said, 'HA!' exceptionally loudly. 'You called Him "He". I thought that wasn't allowed?'

And pinstripes was like, 'Oh, grow up.'

And I said, 'Gentlemen, gentlemen…'

Just at that moment… Oh, it's barely worth saying. I wanted to say something like, 'What is the point of trying to create great work when your shit work is considered just as good?' But what could I say? It was St Paul's. After this I would be famous. And dance with the Devil as that was, I thought, 'After this I can really foist something meaningful on the world.' I felt immanent.

The Church. Like throughout history, all that the art owned by the Church proved is that it was the Church that had stolen the money from the peasants to pay for the bloody art. All art, of them times, anyway, had a blood-red taint in that way.

I was seeing red all the way back to King's Cross Station in the taxi, and all the way in the train back to Glasgow. But walking back from Central Station to my studio I calmed down to contemplative, though I felt far from miraculous and heavenly. I found Douglas sitting on my doorstep, reading something on a piece of paper in his hand, or mibby he was making notes. I couldn't quite see. It was dark. And he said, 'Well? How did it go?'

And I said, 'How long have you been sitting here?' It was about nine o'clock at night.

And he said, 'A wee while. I wanted to find out how it went. And I had nothing else to do.'

And I said, 'We're artists. We've always got something else to do.'

And he said, 'Well, nothing I could be bothered doing. How did it go?'

And I said, 'Well, it went.'

And he said, 'Aye, but good? Good went or bad went?'

And I said, 'It's St Paul's. How could it be bad?'

And he said, 'Aye? Good.'

And I said, 'Do you fancy going for a drink?'

And he said, 'Aye? Aye, sure.'

When we got sat down in the pub and got some drinks in I said to him, 'Do you fancy staying over tonight and then we can get started early tomorrow morning? I want to work in morning light.'

And he said, 'The morra? Aye, I don't think there's anything on the morra I can be bothered doing.' And then he paused and thought, and then he said, 'Except modelling for you, that is.'

And I said, 'Thanks.'

And he said, 'You want to get cracking on the painting you're going to do for St Paul's, eh?'

And I said, 'Yes. Yes, I do.'

Next morning, when we'd finished eating some scrambled eggs and toast, I said to him, 'How about now? Are you ready to get going?'

And he said, 'Aye, sure, why no?'

We went through into the studio and he got up on the trolley, turned round and spread out his arms, waiting for me to bind his arms to the cross-beam. I got up on the ladder and started working the bindings and rope round and round. The bindings were so that the rope wasn't against his skin and the ropes were the necessary strength for weight bearing. We had learned that the bindings and the ropes needed to be tight for him to be able to stand any length of time up there, though more than anything the wee perch that allowed him to rest his weight on was what added minutes, sometimes up to fifteen or more minutes, that gave us a forty-five minute or even an hour-long single session of painting before I had to unbind him and let him rest. Usually another session within that day was just about possible, but sometimes not, though that had more to do with my loss of motivation than his.

I moved the trolley away from him, and though he winced and made little adjusting movements, I knew that he was more or less as comfortable as he could be. I looked at the knots in the bindings and rope. And I said, 'Are you OK?'

He didn't reply by speaking, but with his eyes tightly shut and his teeth bared he nodded briefly and made a strained 'mmn' noise. I stared at him then for a good long while, ten minutes or more, mibby. I was shuffling things around, paint buckets, the canvas a couple of times, walking back and forth the small distance between him and the canvas, looking up at him, looking at the ropes and bindings again. All this time his eyes were tightly shut. I imagined he was concentrating on not feeling pain.

And I said, 'I'll be a minute.' He said nothing.

I wasn't quite sure what I was doing. I sort of watched myself walk out of the studio and close the door over and then I was looking at the key in the lock and my hand twisting it and feeling the lock throw. And then I was turning into my flat, walking through the hall and into my bedroom, filling a bag with a few pairs of knickers and a couple of t-shirts and another pair of shoes. Then it was like *nouvelle vague* jump cuts. Me at the front door, just about able to hear him calling out my name. On a train to Oban. On the jetty. The wind blowing in my face on the ferry. The warmth of my faither's car. Sitting with my mithair by the fire. How many hours had passed? Seven? Seven, mibby. It was late and I was heading off to bed, and, although I was still thinking about Douglas, he wasn't what I dreamed about. Whenever I'm on the island I always dream about the sea. The depth of the sea. The darkness of the sea at night. The hideousness of the sea, and how the sea should be feared.

Three nights later I retraced my steps. The hearth, the car, Oban, the train, Glasgow, the studio. And Douglas. I arrived about nine o'clock again and half expected him to be sitting on my doorstep again. I'm not afraid to admit that my hand trembled as I threw the lock of the door to the studio. Only then I realised there was no light in there. Dear God. Not only had I done this to him, left him hanging there for three days and three nights, but I had left him, half the time, in the dark.

His head was bowed. His body sagged, as much as the bindings and the rope would allow. Douglas was in a horrific state, without doubt dehydrated and starving. For a moment I thought I had killed him. Three days and three nights. I imagined his screaming. But there was no one close by to hear screaming. Sandyford was still a God-forsaken site at this time. And had he had the energy to scream? To call out? To whimper?

I knew that he must have slept little, though passed out many times from searing muscle pain. I put a light on. He stirred, but not much. He was just exhausted. Something vital, an internal organ, seemed to have moved down from under his ribcage to sit horribly bulging from his side. Ended. Finished. The marks of urine and excrement down the etched lines of strain in his legs to his feet. I stood staring in an awful, transfixed horror. Douglas stared down from a sweat-drenched face that had lost all human expression, the face of an animal which knows only pain and suffering.

And he whispered, 'Pain…'

He mustered his strength and whispered again, 'Pain…'

His parched throat. His lips cracked. The pleading in his eyes as he said, 'Pain…'

His torso had begun to sag in a really unnatural way and his spine was in a strange twisted alignment. He nodded – a tiny nod – to move his head a millimetre was torture, and his eyes flickered… no, flicked in a certain direction.

I didn't understand him until his eyes had managed to flick in the direction of his meaning. Buckets and pots of paint I had left three days and nights before on the floor before him. Looking up at him the whole time I leaned down and swished a cane in the paint.

And he said, 'Pain…'

I took a paintbrush from a pot close by.

And he said, 'Pain… Pain…'

And I said, 'I know. I know. Yes.'

And I began to paint, like he wanted me to. And I painted. God forgive me. I painted.

Later on we found out he had a hernia of the diaphragm and a prolapsed liver.

X

If you can't believe it, then believe you me, I couldn't believe it either. The way I had treated him, the way he had accepted being treated. I had tortured him and he had just accepted it. I was as shocked as anyone by his actions, but, of course, most of all by my own. What had I been thinking? What had I been *doing*? The sheer immorality of it. The utter debasedness of it. I was so sorry for him, for Douglas. And yet he was still willing to come back and work with me on my Crucifixion.

And I said, 'No, it's over. Don't you think so? I'm too crazy. And you're too crazy to contemplate continuing.'

And he said, 'We're so close.'

And I said, 'Yes, *too* close. Are you wired to the moon, pal?'

Even a year later, I think I was still in shock by the way I had treated him, by my capacity for hurting Douglas, and for what? The pursuit of the perfect depiction of Christ on the cross? The increasingly distressing images I had gained from increasingly physically distressing Douglas: what was it for? Was it for the art, or was it something to do with me and Douglas? I'm not sure I could have told you. I'm not sure he could have, either.

I asked him and he just shrugged and said, 'It was what it was. I think it was for the art. Right?'

That path to the cross was over. It had all ended as the usual thick treacly paint abstract anyway. I had a theory about why that kept happening. I'll tell you later.

So, in an attempt much more like the original conception of an almost anodyne westernised perfection painting, like something the Vatican would mass-produce, and having done my usual of going back to look at the *Christ of St John of the Cross* by Dalí, and – most important of all – having promised Douglas I wouldn't mistreat him like I had done ever again, I set to work. He came over twice that year to model and I spent the rest of the time working on it alone. This was going to be the one, the final one – if this one didn't work, that was it, I had said.

And he said, 'You're sure?'

And I said, 'This's it.'

And he was like, 'Aye? Well, OK then.'

And the result? Another overworked abstract in black and blue and ochre and yellow. As we stood and looked at it, dismayed, Douglas said, 'Is it me or is it…?'

And I said, 'It is, isn't it? Jesus Christ.'

And he was like, 'Mibby we're just getting used to them.'

And I was like, 'No. It's there for all to see. My God. Can you believe it?'

And he was like, 'I don't know what to say. I don't know why it is.'

And I said, 'It doesn't matter why it looks bland and bleurgh. It matters that it is.'

And he said, 'Yes, but,' he moved his head to his right shoulder, 'how does it… I mean, you said you were shooting for anodyne…'

And I was like, 'Douglas, I can't talk about this right now.'

And he was like, 'Aye? Aye. OK.'

All the faults of the previous attempts at the Crucifixion were laid so bare. You should have seen how drunk we got that night. And I was a slurry mess as I told him, 'New plan No more Crrruucifuxion. That's it.'

Of course that wasn't it. Of course I didn't stick to that plan. Even as he was leaving to go back to New York I was half capitulating, at least to the idea that I would see him again next year.

And he was like, 'Sure, Susan Alison. Whatever happens we'll still meet up, get together. You're about the only person in the art world back here I have anything to do with and would have anything to do with.'

And I don't know why, but I said, 'Oh? Why's that?'

And he said, 'I don't know, it just is what it is.'

And I was like, 'Was what it was, is what it is… you're getting awful philosophical about things in your old age.'

And he was like, 'Aye? Aye, that's me, so it is.'

So, when he came back over the next year, I had no canvas prepped, as we just weren't going to do it. Instead I had made tea and cakes and set it all up in the kitchen, not the studio. We could just sit and talk, I thought, when he came to see me. When I opened the door to him he looked more radiant and beautiful than ever, and

153

his temples showed a wee bit of grey and his hair would soon be going salt and pepper all over, you could see.

I think it was because it was a kitchen table between us rather than model on cross and painter with paintbrush, or because it looked like I was going to stick to my plan of abandoning the Crucifixion, or because I was married now (I know that a spouse has arrived in this story with the equivalence of a kitchen table you didn't know so far that I had, but this story isn't about the spouses any more than it's about the table), but that afternoon we got to talking about all sorts of things from the past, about when we were young and I was first painting him and he was getting famous for his urine art.

And he said, 'Aye. Naked ambition, back then, wasn't it?'

Anyway, it took ages to get on to the Crucifixion, which, OK, it was bound to come up eventually.

And he said, 'Was it me? I was wrong for it, mibby?'

And I said, 'No. How can you think that?'

And he said, 'I just think… I just think if I had done something different, or been someone different, you would have been able to… Uch, I don't know. Just let me blame myself, OK? Because I can't blame you.'

And I was like, 'You are kidding, aren't you? It's me that reworks them and reworks them. You've even told me to just stop, and do I listen?'

And he was like, 'It was me, Susan Alison. Let yourself off. It was me.'

We were silent for a while and then finally I said, 'Patrick!'

And Douglas was like, 'What?'

And I said, 'Patrick, your pal Patrick. When he stood in for you for that year it was the same deal. I messed it up just the same way as ever when he was Jesus instead of you.'

And Douglas was like, 'Aye, well, OK, a wee bit harder for me to martyr myself, then.'

Again we were silent, then Douglas goes, 'What was it like with him, anyway? I've never thought to ask.'

And I said, 'Yes. Well. It didn't work out. He was a wee bit...'

And Douglas was like, 'What? Was he a wee bit creepy? Because he can be like that with women.'

And I said, 'Yes. Well. He was a wee bit sleazy, yes.'

And Douglas said, 'Sleazy? Jeez. How?'

And I said, 'Oh, just his chat was a wee bit... He thought you and I were sleeping together, convinced himself. And mibby he thought that was part of the deal.'

And Douglas said, 'Really? I never said anything to him, by the way, that would make him think—'

And I said, 'Don't worry. I know.'

And Douglas said, 'Sleazy? Wow. I'm really sorry.'

And I said, 'It wasn't your fault. He was just, you know, "Paint me naked." He wanted to kick up controversy. Said I should paint him with a hard-on, a "storkie", he called it. He said he could, you know, that he'd be OK if a big hard-on was required...'

And Douglas was like, '*What*? Jesus God.'

And I said, 'Yes, he said that we look at the cross, and we think, "Jesus, we could all end up like that," and the first thing we are looking for is lumber. Storkies. Lumbers. He has a way of sweet talking, that guy.'

Douglas looked furious, then started laughing.

155

And I started laughing too and said, 'He had some theory that Jesus is actually a fertility god symbol, something
like that, and that he should have this huge erection.'

Douglas was laughing harder.

And I went on, 'Well, I guess he was right that I would
have got into all sorts of trouble about blasphemy and bad
taste – I'd have disgusted the public and transgressed public
morals and there would have been a public execution
of me in George Square, burnt at the stake like St Joan.
I suppose he would have gotten me famous… or infamous.
I mean, once you get that idea into your head… Jesus with
a hard-on.'

And he said, 'Christ.'

And I said, 'And everyone was a girl. This girl and that
girl.'

And he said, 'Oh God, and of course you hate that.
Because of the huts.'

And I said, 'Mmm.'

And he said, 'Are you going to tell me that story? Ever?'

And I said, 'Yes. One of these days.'

And he said, 'Aye? Aye, right.'

After a while we went on drinking our tea. My husband
came in for a moment and said he heard we were having a
rare old time together and I introduced Douglas and him
to each other and my husband embarrassed me by saying
several times, 'Wow, *the* Douglas, *the* Douglas.' I think he
meant *my* the Douglas, but it's possible Douglas thought
he meant *the* Douglas MacDougal, *the* big rich and famous
'piss' artist. But my husband is a musician, works for BBC
SSO, and he doesn't really know or care much about art or
artists. He meant *my* the Douglas.

When my husband had gone back up the stair I said, 'Mibby he was right about one thing.'

And Douglas said, 'Who?'

And I said, 'Patrick.'

And Douglas said, 'Aye? What?'

And I said, 'I should have given the naked Christ a shot. I was always angry about Eric Gill backsliding from the naked Christ he did. And, come on, no one being eviscerated and flogged half to death before being crucified keeps a dignified wee loincloth on, does he? It's such a lie and we were such liars for keeping to that tradition. I was. It was wicked, really. Mibby it was just that, that I was always lying, that I couldn't lay Christ bare, and because of that I always failed.'

And Douglas was like, 'You know, Willem Dafoe's naked in *The Last Temptation*, and the Jesus in that Canadian film we saw, but whatever. But the loincloth? That's what did it, was it?'

And I was like, 'You know what I mean. It's lying about *God*. It's what makes religion safe when it should be dangerous, what makes art *lies* when it should be about the *truth*. Every painting, sculpture and film still lies about the loincloth – we cannot, for all the violence of the Passion, lay the final indignity upon Jesus, that *of course* he would have been flogged naked and crucified naked. *That's* the morality of Christianity. Show a man, have as your defining symbol him as he bleeds and dies, but for God's sake don't show his *genitals*, as though he was some sort of pagan Greek. That would be going too far. And then the lie of art on top of that, that the depiction of the man on the cross must be of beautiful and heartbreaking and exquisite

157

suffering, tasteful enough to be acceptable so the priests and brides of Christ and the patrons and the matrons of the Church didn't get their panties in a twist from looking at a cock.'

Douglas had started to smile through my wee diatribe and I stopped and smiled too and said, 'What?'

And he said, 'You know.'

And I said, 'What?'

And he said, 'You *know*. You know what *has* to happen now.'

And I said, 'Right, mister, get naked.'

You know, these were the years when Peter Doig, whose work I love, was coming to recognition, and I was always on the lookout for opportunities to see his paintings, which meant travelling to this or that gallery. And like wee tips I had had for Scottie Wilson and Alan Davie before him, I was willing to go pretty far to see Doig's stuff. And that's how it happened. How I came to be in the gallery when it happened. I turned a corner and there it was. Not a Doig. I had been misinformed about there even being Doigs in exhibition in this gallery. I turned a corner and there it was. And by this time, I had seen them all, the Grünewald and the Peter Paul Rubens and the van Dyck and the Velázquez, the Batoni, the ghostly Blake, the Bouguereau, Ge, Emil Nolde and Marc Chagall's *White Crucifixion* and *Yellow Crucifixion* and Georges Rouault's and Sieger Köder's *Holocaust* from his *Stations of the Cross*, and of course Dalí's two Crucifixions, Robert Henderson Blyth's utterly despairing *Image of Man*, and Bacon's we've already discussed, and James Dickson Innes's 1913

one where Jesus and the thieves are high, high up on tall
crosses, and Jones's and Weight's and Sutherland's and de
Maistre's and Elliot's and Tintoretto's and Sano di Pietro's
gushing blood one and Roberts's and Wagner's 1993 one
and Anton Lehmden's 1965 one and John Reilly's one
from 1962, Rauschenberg's *Panel 107* and Alex Guy's Elvis
one, Stanley Spencer's and Gilbert Spencer's, Aitchison's
innumerable Crucifixions, and every one in between, and
these are just the paintings, and I'm sure you'll notice the
other thing about them all. If you don't get me, try putting
something like 'Depictions of the Crucifixion by women
artists' in a search engine and you'll soon find out. What
you get is, apart from loads of women *in* depictions of the
Crucifixion, Mary and mother Mary and Martha and the
like, are hundreds of images of women being crucified.
It never gets to the Sarah Lucas ones. But anyway, I had
thought deeply about them all and tried to sort through the
meaning of each and the emphasis of each and why what
I could do and how I could do it to stamp my emphasis
and my meaning on a new painting of the Crucifixion
would make it worthwhile as an addition to the art of the
cross and make it worthy of being in this lineage. And I
turned a corner and there was Norman Adams's 1993
watercolour *The Golden Crucifixion*. In the painting Christ
is on the cross, but he has also been a caterpillar who is
now emerging from his chrysalis and his wings are unfol-
ded. The transformation is complete, the transfiguration
of Christ from a radiant man into a golden God. My
God. I felt like I was sinking deep, deep into an ocean of
black. This was the painting I had been trying to paint.
This was it. I wept. It was so beautiful. I wept and went

back to the sad little bed and breakfast I was staying in that night. I did not eat and went to bed early. But I did not sleep. In a way, I felt I was in my own Garden of Gethsemane. I fell to some deep, dark place in my mind where there was nothing and nothing and nothing always. Like I had died and gone to hell and, becoming conscious I was in hell, realising that it was exactly the place I had just left, this room, this bed and breakfast, this night after seeing *The Golden Crucifixion*. And, in some way, it has been Gethsemane nightly for me ever since, whenever I think about Adams's beautiful painting.

I remember now. I said, 'What does it mean, anyway, the Crucifixion?'

This was part of the God-lives-in-heaven story I was telling you earlier. Sorry, I'm getting out of sequence now.

And Douglas said, 'They nail them up.'

And I said, 'I don't mean that way. I mean, what does it mean, the Crucifixion of Jesus?'

And he said, 'Oh, I don't know what to say. He died that we might live.'

And I said, 'Yes. What does that mean?'

And he said, 'To conquer death?'

And I said, 'Yes, what does that mean? People still die.'

And he said, 'Only so that they live on in the Kingdom of Heaven.'

And I said, 'Yes, what does that mean?'

And he said, 'He died to take away the sins of the world.'

And I said, 'God! What does *that* mean? Take away the sins of the world? Was there no more sinning after him? Don't think so. And heaven. What is heaven?'

And he said, 'To live on close to God. To see God. Not in hell.'

And I said, 'Oh, mibby we're getting somewhere. Not in hell, indeed! And are we in heaven?' I struck my breastbone and said, 'We, us, this?'

And he said, 'What, our bodies? No. Our souls. Our souls are in heaven.'

And I said, 'Right, right. So we know this, do we? We are us, ourselves, in heaven?'

And he said, 'I don't think so. Our souls are there, close to God. Seeing God.'

And I said, 'Do you believe any of this stuff?'

And he said, 'Do you?'

And I said, 'I asked first.'

And he said, 'What's to believe? I haven't even heard a coherent description. From anyone. Not a priest or a minister or a Hare Krishna. None of them. No one can describe the big man or where the hell he lives. Not in a way I can understand.'

And I said, 'You're so pretty when you're empty.'

And he said, 'Thanks. I'm a naïve artist. Primitive.' He made gestures.

And I said, 'Um… you're a monkey… you're a monkey sculpting… no! Painting! You're a monkey painting… abstracts, or throwing paint, or throwing faeces! You're a Fauvist throwing faeces of exploding colours on to the bland canvas of the stale establishment of fin de siècle Paris!'

And he said, 'Nice.' He was nodding. And he said, 'What about heaven?'

And I said, 'Oh, what about it? Who cares these days? Heaven is a place with unending Fry's Chocolate Creams. That, if it is anything.'

And he said, 'Fry's?'

And I said, 'My mithair. I asked her once what heaven was like and she said, "Well, I like Fry's Chocolate Creams. So, when I get to heaven, there'll be as many Fry's Chocolate Creams as I want, and there will be no end to Fry's," and I said "But I don't like Fry's Chocolate Creams." And she said, "Don't be stupid, Susan Alison, that'll be how *I* experience heaven. You'll experience it your way and whatever it is you want and love and need will be there." And I said, "Will you be there, Mummy?" And she said, "Well, just look out for the piles and piles of Fry's." And then she sent me to bed. Happy, I might add.'

And he said, 'Might you?'

And I said, 'I might. She also said that when you turf up in heaven, meeting St Peter at the gates, you are in your prime, the perfect version of yourself, which she pegged at age forty. I think this was even true if you were under forty, in childhood, even, when you died.'

And he said, 'Aye? My mother used to say that, too. You showed up in heaven in the prime of your life. Unless you were one of the wee babies in limbo or one of the to-be-prayed-for souls in purgatory. In purgatory you were just the age you were when you died. Funny, she never said anyone went to hell, though. Except mibby for "Hell mend ye", I don't remember her mentioning hell at all.'

And I said, 'We didn't have limbo and purgatory. But we had hell, all right. Definitely a lot of hell going around.'

And he said, 'Look, I don't even get the resurrection. Jesus dies. He's telling the good thief—'

And I said, 'Who?'

And he said, 'The good thief. The bad thief and the good thief, either side of him, getting crucified—'

And I said, 'Oh. Yes.'

And he said, 'Jesus, he's telling the good thief, the repentant or penitent one, or whatever you'd call him, "Tonight you will be with me in paradise." So, he's going to heaven, Jesus and this thief. But then Jesus goes and arises from the dead.'

And I said, 'Well, that's resurrection for you.'

And he said, 'Yes, but then he's alive again? On earth instead of in paradise? Bad deal, right?'

And I said, 'Well... Eh. Huh?'

And he said, 'Exactly. Why come back? This is just earth. What's so great about here in comparison to paradise? Just smacks of, you know, superstition of a tribe. Coming alive again... miraculous! Why? Because life is good and meaningful. He died to fulfil a prophecy. He couldn't save himself. Why? Why didn't he just tell his disciples the stuff he came back to tell them before? In fact, he did, he didn't say anything momentous after or different from before. What's so great about resurrection to a son of God? Nothing. Impressive to the alive at the time, but in terms of the story—'

And I said, 'Well, it means... means... well—'

And he said, 'Exactly. What? What does it mean? Anyway, he ascends into paradise, into heaven, at the end, anyway. So that's OK. Because paradise is better, up there,' and he gestured, 'with God. Right? Am I right?'

I might have nodded. I was thinking, St Peter, you know, you're St Peter and you're thinking, how the hell did *I* end up the guy at the Pearly Gates? And then I was thinking it would have been like, 'Oh right, because I was handed the keys of heaven,' like you say. You know in Matthew chapter 16, verse 18 Jesus said, 'I tell you that you are Peter, and on this rock I will build my Church, and the gates of Hades will not overcome it.' And in verse 19 Jesus was like, 'I will give you the keys of the Kingdom of Heaven.' All that so you end up the gatekeeper. And you're left thinking, 'It's not a great gig, but it's a living.'

And Douglas said, 'It just all kind of strikes me as, well, aye, OK, it makes sense, the Gospels and that, looked at as something coming from a few wee villages and towns in the dark of two millennia ago, in fear and trembling, scared to death of death and unable to think that… that this can't be it. So they need this anti-death cult or something. They just can't accept—' And he paused then said, 'But as a worldview two thousand years on, as a world religion, it just seems like the facts don't fit thegether, the stories just don't work.'

And I said, 'Well, cults, that's something you'd know about.'

And he said, 'Aye? What do you mean by that?'

And I said, 'You must have noticed. The way people look at you when we're out and about in the West End. They look at you. You're a bit of a cult yourself. The Cult of Douglas.'

And he said, 'What? Are you joking?'

And I said, 'Well, they look at you behind your back. You can't see. I can.'

And he was like, 'I think you're a wee bit off the mark.'

And I was like, 'No. I'm right. You're a cult now.'

And he said, 'Aye? OK. How do you think I can exploit that?'

And I said, 'Nice.'

And he said, 'Hey, come on. You know that's what it's about. The Gospel According to Me. I kind of like that. The Lord is out of control!'

And I said, 'They look at you as though they're trying to see through your clothes, through your skin, through your flesh, to see what's inside you.'

And he said, 'Naw. Come on. Really?'

And I said, 'Well... Man, check out the Tolstoy *Gospel in Brief*. I was waiting for the searing Crucifixion scene and it's like done in, "So, anyway, yadda yadda yadda, he died." I mean, *what*?'

And he said, 'You can't always expect too much from the artist, Susan Alison.'

And I said, 'Which artist? I certainly don't expect too much from you.' And suddenly I flared into a red-hot flame of bad temper and I said, 'You are not an artist. You're a drunk that happens to get work in galleries. There is a difference.'

And he said nothing for a while, then, 'OK. Aye. Well, that sounded like the naked truth.'

And you know the end of this story by now. Of course you do. Like the ones I've told you about, and the ones I have skipped telling you about: the sun and moon one; the one where Douglas is sitting down in front of the cross holding a trout; the ones with the secondary figures (not many of them – I always was happiest when I was painting the most isolated of Christs); the one with the small children in the background; the one where I tried leaning the sleeper upright forward because I was going for the Dalí viewpoint in *Christ of St John of the Cross* (the pain which this caused Douglas in one session made him puke, and I thought for a moment of just keeping painting and adding the puking into the picture – Jesus was a *human*, and wouldn't being flogged and nailed up make any of us puke, piss ourselves, shit ourselves); the one with him dripped head to foot in blood (fake, this time); the double one; and the ones Douglas named, like the one he named the 'after the flood' one, and the Stanley Kubrick one, the ghost-nets one, the fridge-magic one, the one that he looked at lying horizontal and said, 'Is it a funeral pyre, do you think?', all of which were painted over and don't exist anymore, thank God; the naked Christ painting, the naked Douglas, failed, ended up a thickened mess of turbulent fleshy waves that was yellow ochre and burnt sienna and raw umber and blackened blue and sickly, yellowing white and blood vermillion.

And he said, 'What was it you were really expecting to happen, Susan Alison? It would have happened anyway.'

XI

We were drifting apart by 1998, me and Douglas. In fact, I don't think I saw him that year, or in 1999. His work increasingly took him abroad, mostly to New York, where he was by then known as Doug Cody, creating ever-more elaborate versions of his urine bags. One filled a huge warehouse space with only a few feet of floor space around the perimeter for visitors to the gallery to view this gigantic sea of urine. It was called *TEN YEARS*. If I remember rightly, much was made of the thickness and quality of the plastic bag used so that the turgidity of the bag is maintained by the immense volume of liquid. I watched a documentary on his work from that time and I remember he spent the whole hour seemingly talking about the plastic bag. Not much mention of where all the urine came from. None, in fact. Kirsty Wark presented and interviewed him as well as some of the members of his army of assistants. Gallery-goers queued for blocks on Manhattan's Upper East Side to see this monolithic new work. One critic said it was the greatest expression of the millennial tension of our times. I mean, how, exactly?

The only contact I remember clearly from 1999 was this gift he sent me, a CD box-sized package arriving in the post with a note written in his weird scrawl, saying, 'Here, take this, I want you to have it. Frankly, you're not going to believe it. I couldn't believe it when one of my pals gave me it to listen to.'

Then there was a phone call to New York, and he was repeating himself, 'You're just not going to believe it.'

'Very mysterious! What are you on about?' I said.

'You'll see… you'll get it when you hear it,' he said.

I looked at the ripped-open wrapping and the two CDs by a Glasgow band called Mogwai, *Come On Die Young* and *Young Team*. I twisted them around in my hands. 'I think I've heard of them,' I said, 'but I haven't heard them. Thanks.'

He said, 'You're going to be amazed, blown away.'

'They're that good? Well, thanks again, that's great,' I said.

'No. I mean, yes, but that's not it,' he said. 'You'll see when you hear.'

'Oh, look, they have a song called 'Cody', like your nickname,' I said.

'Aye,' he said, 'but that's not it.'

I put the CDs on in the studio a couple of times as I painted during the days that followed this phone call, but I kept getting to the end of each CD and realised I hadn't really been listening, resolving to listen more closely the next time I played them. But it was a few months before I called him in New York again, having finally worked out what was going on. 'It's just plain weird,' I said.

'No kidding,' he said.

'I must have heard the Iggy Pop thing years ago or something, the one they use on 'Punk Rock',' I said.

'I suppose that's possible,' he said.

'And I suppose I must have heard their other stuff without realising, and then I go repeating their words when I'm in my... during my seizures,' I said.

'But the way I remember some of the things – you were saying them before Mogwai were recording them songs,' Douglas said.

'No, you must be mixed up, about the years of things, events,' I said. 'I mean, how can I have been saying those things before they recorded them?'

'Well, that's the way I remember it happening,' he said. 'Some of the stuff you were saying was in nineteen eighty-eight. That's three or four years before the band even formed.'

'No,' I said. 'Come on. Mibby the Iggy Pop speech was one I was repeating in nineteen eighty-eight. And I could have heard that well before nineteen eighty-eight.'

'No the way I'm remembering it,' he said.

'Well, I suppose, I mean, anyway, my memory of my seizures,' I said, 'it isn't as good as yours...'

'But I'm telling you,' he said, 'it's verbatim, what you said, what's on their albums. Identical.'

I said, 'But how could it be?'

'I don't know what to say. Start recording yourself during seizures,' he said. 'We'll see if you say anything that's on their music next year or whenever.'

'That's an idea,' I said.

Though, I have to admit I haven't ever bothered to do that. I mean, the premise is just so unbelievable. Somehow in my seizures I say words and hear music that finds its way into songs by Mogwai? I don't know of any theory of hallucinations that would account for that psychologically. I also don't know of any religious belief or even supernatural or paranormal phenomenon that would explain why I would be somehow composing and transmitting songs to a band from Glasgow. What would be the point, apart from anything else? The one thing that seems to somehow give some framework for what seemed to be happening is that thing about time moving backwards that physicists say is the way the world will end. They say something like that, don't they? I think they do, anyway. Do they? Something about remembering the future as you plunge back down through the past as the universe collapses. Though, come to think of it, there are the precogs in that film, the Philip K. Dick story, they know stuff before the things happen. But it has to be important stuff, doesn't it? Like a murder or something. And, as much as you might love Mogwai, and I do, I don't think their songs would be precogged by the precogs. Again, what exactly would be the point? And, of course, now I'm thinking how I'm showing myself up for the heathen I am, the atheist, because the phenomenon that it's really like, isn't it, is that I was like a prophet. Prophecy is all in the saying what the future holds. But Mogwai tunes? What kind of prophecy is that? It's not exactly the time and date of the Apocalypse. Not unless, you know, you've seen them do 'Mogwai Fear Satan' live.

Being shown up is one of my mithair's things, by the way. 'Oh, Susan Alison, you've shown yourself up again...' To be honest, I don't really understand it, this prophecy thing, and I just say it's something freaky about the seizures themselves, a fluke, something that is weird *apparently* because it's not really real.

So, anyway, and this's going to become important in a minute or two, but for the Crucifixion I had gone back to oil paints. I mean, gouache acrylics? Come on. It had to be oils. In the end it had to be. You always end up where you started from.

The next time I got Douglas up on the cross (which is also, come on, you knew this was going to be the way it was) I remember he was saying something about the Passion actually built from passion, with passion, mad passion, passion to the extreme. Something like that, anyway. 'Mmhm,' I said as I bound his naked body, arms, wrists, legs, ankles, to the cross.

He went on speaking. Again, something about passion, or the Passion. Something about his mother. Something about her saying, 'Jesus, Mary and Joseph!' and how one of his brothers said that he always thought there were nine kids in the family because the six names of the six actual kids in the family, when shouted, were always followed by 'Jesus, Mary and Joseph!' Something about New York. He was telling me about how, in New York, being out of his element, critics kept saying things about his Calvinist spirit, his protestant work ethic and all the rest. 'Because I'm Scottish and they think of Scotland as a Proddy country,' he said, looking into the space in front of him, up there on the cross.

'Well, I suppose it is,' I said.

He looked down at me. 'And if I was Irish they'd assume I was Catholic. And when I tell them I am Catholic, well, brought up Catholic, they then – get this – ask if I'm Irish, even when they know I'm Scottish,' he said.

'They mean Scots-Irish, or Irish-Scots or... Americans should know all about all this, especially in New York,' I said.

He said, 'Aye? Aye. I'm just out of my element, for them, that's all.' Then he said, 'Why is it I finally feel so comfortable up here? This is no bother at all.'

'Mmhm,' I said a few times over as I got the ladder and the big nails for the big canvases and the big hammer for hammering the big nails.

When I got up on the ladder and kind of above him, he knew it was coming, and ever so quietly, as my face passed close to his face as I stretched out the nail and hammer to his right wrist, then his palm, then his wrist again, he said, 'We can talk about this.'

'You think?' I said.

'Aye. Yes. Eh. Aye. Sure. We can talk,' he said.

'Yes?' I said.

'Look, Suse. I know what you're doing here,' he said. His breathing was getting a wee bit rapid.

'Mmhm,' I said.

'I have followed your line,' he said.

'Yes,' I said.

'I'm with you,' he said.

I went, 'Mmhm.'

'So we can talk?' he said.

'No, I don't think so,' I said.

172

'I think we can, Susan Alison,' he said.

I noticed he was sweating really profusely. Quite disgusting, really. His body was giving off this really unusual smell, too.

'We can,' he repeated.

'Look, I think it's best if we just get on with this,' I said. The nail was on his flesh now. I was digging it in, ready for the hammer.

'Jesus, Suse. Susan Alison, I really think we can talk about this. Just give us a wee bit of time to talk about this,' he said.

I thought for a second. Then I shook my head. 'It's better this way. You know we've got to create something good,' I said. 'Something that will last. I mean… Shush… quiet now… shush… Be a man.' I raised the hammer.

He was screaming something, like, 'Suse-no-wait-we-can-we-*can-talk-it DOESN'T-SUSE!-SUSE!*—'

The hammer fell and there was a squishing then a crunchy breaking sound.

'…It's for the art,' I said, as though I had just understood what it was that was necessary for the art, which mibby I had. I was whispering. He was screaming; sounds now, not words.

The hammer rose again and fell and WHAM – the second blow did seem to drive the nail through to the railway sleeper below his hand.

XII

I'm not sure whether I can explain the next thing that happened very well. As I poised the nail over his left wrist and poked around, looking for somewhere the nail would go through without hitting bone again, then moved it to the palm of his left hand and poked around there – he was making a lot of screaming noises at this point, but then I don't think I could hear him any more – his hand, the palm of his hand, grew bigger. At first I thought it was just my skewed perspective in my concentrated focus on this palm of his hand, poking at his skin and flesh trying to see and feel where the way through was without having to drive the nail through bone, which I didn't feel totally confident I could do again, and I knew that his hand had grown bigger, by now to almost double its normal size, four times its normal size, mibby. I really whammed the hammer down on the nail and the bloody thing, the nail, went bent such that I couldn't hit down on it again and I was like, 'Oh, buggeration,' because there would be no way of salvaging that one, but I just got another nail and right next to the one all skewed and

175

pointless and unsaveable I carefully, this time, tapped it in and then thwacked it on into his wrist. And still it, his wrist, everything in my sight line, was growing larger and larger, except it was difficult to tell because everything else in my focus was also increasing in size at the same rate. The palm of his hand, his arm, him, the cross, me, the studio. It was all growing at this phenomenal rate, and yet it was difficult to watch it happening, because everything was remaining in perfect scale, so it wasn't my perspective that was off. It must have been something else. And I was wondering whether mibby everything in the world that was not in my focus – Glasgow outside this studio, Scotland, the world itself – was it growing, or was it staying the same? And if the world outside the studio was not growing like we were growing, were Douglas and I and the cross and the studio going to, what's the word, engulf Sandyford, then Glasgow, then Scotland, then somehow become this immense studio with an immense cross and artist and model inside, in scale to the immenseness of itself, which would finally, I don't know, tip the balance of the earth on its axis, unbalance the rotation of the world and have us spin out of our own orbit round the sun and go crashing into the moon and then spin off into the immenseness of the firmament? And we would just keep getting more and more immense, mibby until even God could see us.

I was thinking, I don't think I have achieved more than this in all my life and career, and I was just so… happy. Filled with joy. Yes. That. My heart was filled to bursting with joy. Like my heart was Douglas's mother's Sacred

Heart of Jesus and there was light within me, shining from my chest and joy, joy, joy.

And then that wasn't what it was like. What it was like was that Douglas and I were slowed down, slowed down to an infinitesimally slow speed, while the world outside us started rushing by in an imperceptibly fast rush, a blur of colour and light like in my faither's favourite episode of the original *Star Trek*, where the landing-party guy and then back on the *Enterprise* Captain Kirk experience time passing normally but find the other lot stood still, though actually they're just moving infinitesimally slowly, while the slowed lot experience Kirk and the aliens as just a kind of high-pitched buzzing fly sound. It was like we were in Douglas Gordon's *24 Hour Psycho*, slowed down to play over twenty-four hours, or, really, some companion piece, *24 Day Psycho*, or *24 Year Psycho*, or, better, *24 Century Psycho*. And I suppose me and Douglas moving the way we were moving was us becoming the picture, the painting, us becoming like all the crucified Jesuses who stare out infinitesimally slowly from their paintings in galleries as the gallery-goers buzz in swarms before them. My faither's favourite was *Star Trek*. My mithair, she liked *The Prisoner*.

In a way, it's like this God and Jesus business, really, isn't it? I mean, where is God? In heaven, mibby, like we've discussed, but we also know for definite that God's in Eternity, that heaven is Eternity in this sense. So, like, for God a human lifetime is like *zzit, zzit*. In fact, not even that. Whole civilisations, like the Mayans or Ancient Greeks, the Romans or Huns or even our own modern civilisation, must just flash – though 'flash' is hardly adequate to express this *b* of the *bang* moment – past God in an almost imperceptible *zzzit, zzzit, zzzit.* God literally does not have time. Some God Squader once told me that trying to figure all this stuff out, trying to figure out the mind of God, was like a bacterium trying to figure out the mind of a human – 'You're just not going to get there' was this God Squader's point. I didn't have any reply then, and just stood there sipping my Kir Royale and probably said something like, 'Mmmm.' But then what does the human know about the bacterium, the individual bacterium? Now I'm thinking that there would have to be some sort of intermediary. And, I've just realised, that's Jesus. God didn't send Jesus down from heaven to earth. Jesus was sent from Eternity in to Time – I suppose so that God could hear all about what the hell was going on in there.

Douglas was whimpering like an animal. I heard him now. I was back at the base of the cross and had obviously finished the job, his ankles nailed separately to each side of the upright sleeper. But the joy had so overwhelmed me that I had no memory of driving the last nails home. I think even at this early stage of the comedown I knew we were not growing ever more huge, not moving slowed down. We were just in the studio and we were in scale with the rest of the world and in normal time. But I could see everything. Everything. The way his skin was taut across his stomach, the twisted spasm of a muscle here, there, his wrenching flesh, the retching in his throat. And the blood – trickles, but still. We were in scale, but I had a sensation that he, the cross, me, the studio, we were ascending, moving upwards, to somewhere high up. And he and the cross were moving up faster than me and the studio.

Here's a strange one for you. Recently, I started reading the Gospels. I know, right? Nutty. You'd have thought that with all this story you've been hearing from me that would have been where I'd have started, not... finished. If this's the end. But it's just that, well, come on, *Jesus of Nazareth* and *The Gospel in Brief* and *The Passion of the Christ* and *The Gospel According to Jesus Christ* and *Jesus Christ Superstar* and *The Last Temptation of Christ* and *The St Matthew Passion* and *The Gospel According to St Matthew* and *Jésus de Montréal*, my God, I had forgotten (The Grosvenor, 1989, *Jésus de Montréal*, Douglas and me). And all the painted depictions of the Crucifixion and all these pieces of art, and a Jesus-freak mum, and the Crucifixion, *his* Crucifixion, being all around us and everywhere, the last place you'd go to find out what went on would be the actual Gospels, right? No? Anyway, it seems it's the last place I've landed.

And what you notice... what *I* noticed in all the Gospels, the three similar ones and then John's, was... well, I was waiting for this scaring, tear-jerking, soul-wrenching Crucifixion. This... words that just... I don't know. And in all of them, all four, this's basically what you get, 'And Jesus was nailed to the cross and then he died. Awful. Mm. Boo hoo. Sad face.'

No kidding, it's that precipitous. I suppose it says that for any of us the end can come quickly. Today. Tomorrow. Whenever.

So, anyway, my art was starting to gain some pretty extravagant praise back then, including that lavished on the major commission for the altar triptych in St Paul's Cathedral. In the end I had given them three of the abstracts that they wanted. What else could I do? There were still four more of them, those abortions, my abortions, and I sold them off at Sotheby's. I should have called them that – a series called *My Abortions*. The St Paul's gig had shot the prices for my work through the roof. Would you believe I made a million? Well, close on a million, before taxes and all that stuff. We bought the house in Sandyford, which until then we had been renting. I didn't sell the last one, the bland one. *My Bland Abortion*. That one I burnt because I couldn't paint over it, the paint was on too thick.

By back then, by 2002 and the last time I painted him as Jesus, Jesus crucified, I had been married for five years and now had a baby boy, and I think I had found contentment in my art without attempting to make the great Crucifixion scene I had always wanted to. Douglas had moved permanently to New York, and I thought he didn't really make it back over to Scotland at all any more. Then, what happened was, I mean it wasn't arranged, I turned another corner in another gallery, my home from home, the Kelvingrove, looking down at my Nokia and a message from him from December ('Mery XMas R U Still in 2 it?'), then looking up, and there he was, standing, wearing these cool European-looking glasses, staring up at Dalí's *Christ of St John of the Cross*.

'Douglas!' I said, and he turned, smiling, to face my smile. 'My God!' I said, 'What are you up to?'

'Oh,' he said, 'just a wee visit to the blessed mother, you know, and the sibs, before travelling to Paris for a show.'

'What show?' I said.

'A solo retrospective,' he said.

'Whose?' I said before thinking.

'Eh, aye, mine,' he said.

That was the one that would guarantee to make him a millionaire several times over and one of the most famous conceptual artists in the world.

He turned back to the painting. He said, 'I was just reading that the painting was damaged, slashed and ripped, in nineteen sixty-one.'

'A very confused young man,' I said, 'Ninian McGregor Menzies, reported as a bearded man. Well, he had to have a beard, didn't he?'

'How?' Douglas said.

'Because of the reason he was attacking the painting,' I said.

Douglas was looking at me over the top rim of his glasses. Every sign of ageing always seemed to make him look more beautiful. Sickening, really.

'He was mentally ill, Ninian,' I said. 'Thought he was Jesus Christ. That's why the beard. And that's why the attack.' I turned to the painting, and Douglas did too. 'Ninian said this painting looked, you know, nothing like him.'

I don't know what led to us reminiscing about our youthful ambitions and desires, but we got there. Mibby this was the typical way we spoke now, for all I knew. I remember him saying at one point, 'Promise, if you ever want to do it, I'll come back to being the model for Jesus on the cross. Is the railway-sleeper cross still in your studio?'

'Sure,' I said, 'I'm an eco-minded modren West End mum. I use reusable nappies for my baby... I hang them to dry on the cross.'

XIII

At the point of his ultimate moment, of his sacrifice to the painting, my painting, my Crucifixion, he reared up, writhed on his cross, tearing flesh and cracking bone, every sinew taut, every muscle tight. And on his face was a look of such abject horror, fear and bewilderment. He howled like a dog. I immediately leaped up, grabbing for my sketchbook. This was it, the look on his face that I had to capture. He looked deep into my eyes as I furiously sketched. This time it would be right. This time I would create a masterpiece. This time I would make a painting that was genuinely, authentically good, no question. Then he was making noises, trying to speak. Whispering. I got up on the ladder and put my ear close to his mouth.

'I wanted it,' he said.

'I know,' I said, 'I know you did.'

When they asked me about Douglas for the profile they did on me for the Turner shortlist, I simply said, 'Now he is immortal and I know that he is happy now that he is immortal.' What else was there to say? It was true.

Douglas told me once that his favourite piece of conceptual art was called *An Oak Tree*, which Michael Craig-Martin put together in 1973. It's a glass of water on what looks like a bathroom shelf, except it's way up on the wall. And there's this text that tells you that what you are looking at is actually an oak tree, a tall, strong oak tree, and my interpretation is that if you have faith and believe that this glass of water on a bathroom shelf is in fact an oak tree then you have understood something essential about the nature of faith and, by extension, the nature of reality. For some people, of course, it's all emperor's new clothes that *An Oak Tree* is really about, taking a pop at the stupidity of people, and of faith, and the artist taking a pop at himself, and conceptual art, and taking a pop at art as a thing in and of itself. Like *Ceci n'est pas une pipe* by Magritte, if you see what I'm saying. I only found out recently that well before Douglas decided on the greatness of *An Oak Tree*, Damien Hirst had long been an advocate of it as the greatest piece of conceptual art ever. I know Douglas was saying it because Damien Hirst had said it first, but did he also think it was true? I mean, he might have, right? He wasn't a liar, Douglas. But he didn't care what was the capital-T Truth either. Well, that's my opinion of him.

Give him his due. As famous as he became, Douglas still did take the time to return to Glasgow to see me, and, if I could stomach it yet one more time, model for Jesus. Although both his visits in 2000, then his next one in 2001, were attended by a circus of media speculation about him and his work and sometimes about our relationship, both professional (which did exist) and personal (which did also exist, we were friends, but, no, it was never like *that*) and friendly or not-so-friendly, amused and not-so-amused gossip among our friends and contemporaries about the need for Douglas to be modelling for abstract depictions of the Crucifixion. Total bloody pandemonium.

The other thing that was happening with me around this time was my synaesthetic visions, as I had come to think of them, had completely left me, which was a relief, but also, in a way, disappointing. I mean, I could do without the freaky feelings and the absences, but I had also lost... *something*. I'm not quite sure what. The hallucinations never really fed into my art. Not like for, you know, Howson and his powerful religious vision, his conversional experience in the year 2000. And as for predicting the band Mogwai's output, well who knows what that was? Coincidence? I remember the writer Frank Kuppner being interviewed on TV, probably by Jenny Brown, who did all that stuff on TV in Scotland back in them days, and Jenny was challenging Frank on his reliance on coincidences in his plots, and Frank says that if there were never *any* coincidences, well, that would be one hell of a big coincidence.

It was never going to work out, that Crucifixion, was the way I had been thinking by that stage. I could never match my conception of the most beautiful, most horrifying, most obscene, most divine and sublime, most sacred and profane image of Christ on the cross ever painted to... to what I was actually doing. That's why more paint and more paint and more paint got added. And probably, in my book, Adams had already got there. Norman Adams, the painter of *The Golden Crucifixion*, remember? Fourteen years on from seeing Douglas at that party in the dark in Hyndland, I knew almost for sure what was wrong. I had been lying to him. It's obvious: Douglas couldn't have ever been the model for Jesus that aligned with my imaginative needs, not until I actually, you know, did it to him, crucified him. I mean, I know this's true. *Why* it's true, that one's a wee bit trickier, trickier business. Well, that I'm just going to have to figure out on my own. Or you work it out for me, then tell me, will you?

Mibby it's like in the art of Islam, which is supposed to have no depictions of Allah, not the way you get a person-God on the Sistine Chapel ceiling, because Allah is just too much, so much bigger than that, than being depicted in a contained form, he's just too *big*. The same then sort of goes for the prophets, Muhammad, and, before him, Jesus, who is a very significant prophet in Islam, if you didn't know this. Like, a mosque wouldn't commission a pictorial depiction of Muhammad the way a church might commission a Crucifixion with a Jesus in it. (My mithair's church had no man on the cross, either, just the cross itself. One of the reasons her denomination was superior to the idolatrous paganism of the Church of Rome. And why she hated me 'talking Glasgow'. No zealot like a convert.) And also in Islam you don't really get a crucifixion and death of Jesus the way you do in Christianity. In some narratives in Islam some other guy gets crucified, mibby one of the disciples, the youngest and bravest, who may be Judas Iscariot. It's not exactly clear, but what is clear is that Jesus at the end of his mission as a prophet on earth ascends into heaven to be with Allah. The point being that whether there is a crucifixion of Jesus or not is unnecessary in Islamic belief. And there's not one in the art of Islam. Where would be the need for an art tradition of the Crucifixion if there's no need for Jesus to be crucified in the first place? And, anyway, Islamic art is always beautiful, never brutal or vicious, never depicting the horror, and sometimes I would like the world to be like that and to be like that myself.

I'd just like to create beautiful art, and not terrifying beauty or horrific beauty, but just beautiful beauty.

Mibby, for all the attempts before the last one, I just couldn't paint something *big enough*. Because that's what you're painting when you're painting the Crucifixion, aren't you? It might not be the orthodox theology, but it is the way that I see it, that Jesus wasn't always there with God, or that he was formed divine when he was conceived of a virgin and born, or when he was transfigured on the mount. The Crucifixion is the end of the man Jesus and the beginning of the God Christ, the Saviour, the Redeemer, the Lord, the Messiah. There's a Ken Currie work in the Kelvingrove called *Untitled*, from 2000, that I think agrees with me. It shows a luminous man, the transfigured Christ, but, essentially, he also has the marks of the Crucifixion on him. Is that what Currie means? That in the moment Jesus dies, that's what he is? Becoming. God coming into the world and sacrificing Himself. And looked at this way, it's a pretty tall order to try to get *that* on canvas. For me, anyway.

I know it might be a cliché, but if I was ever considering going back to a religion, it would be, like for Sinéad O'Connor, who I read recently said it was the inevitable conclusion for any serious theologian, Islam. I know, I know. But she's right, Sinéad. You have to end up where the world has ended up. Anything else is just sun-worshipping and not noticing that Jesus is over there, carrying his cross. Though I have news for any religion of the present, which is that, if humanity survives, then in a hundred or a thousand or three thousand years, something else will have happened. Either science and humanism, or some other prophet will have come along to start an even better religion, mibby something with a goddess

as well as a god, say. That all just has to happen. History
tells us. The end times are coming, just not yet and not for
a while. We have millennia yet. Millennia and millennia.
I saw Sinéad once, in the Pink in Dublin. A nightclub. She
was dancing with Kenny Rogers. Wait. Kenny Rogers and
Sinéad dancing? Now I really am babbling, adding stuff
that doesn't need to be here. I need to watch that. I should
mention out of respect that Sinéad is now called Shuhada'
Sadaqat, her Muslim name.

There's this nice passage in Hadith 5772, by the way, that
says that Muhammad is neither too tall nor too short. He was,
in fact, the perfect height. I'm pegging that at exactly six feet
tall. And he was handsome, beautiful, the most beautiful man.
And if you also want a beautiful portrait of Jesus, read the
one in the Qur'ān. It is so beautiful. Better than the portrait
in the Bible. And in the Qur'ān Jesus's title is not the Good
Shepherd or the Lamb of God or Rabbi or Master or the Son
of Man, and certainly not the Son of God or the Son in the
Trinity – these can't be titles for him, because in the Qur'ān
he's not divine, he's a *man*. In the Qur'ān he is, for the most
part, Jesus the Son of Mary, of Maryam, and I like that. And
I like that moments after being born Jesus can miraculously
speak, and he says he brings this good book, this message
from Allah to His people. Also in Islam there is no worship
but the worship of Allah. And I think that must be just such a
relief for him, for Jesus. Jesus must feel really relieved being a
prophet in Islam. I mean, who'd want that responsibility? To
be worshipped? What I mean is, that can't be fun.

XIV

After things had gone quiet and it seemed like there was nothing else left to do, I got tools and got the nails out of his hands and ankles and carefully unbound him. I lifted him down from the cross. I know. Me, five foot nothing and him a six-footer. But he had grown so slight, never really regained weight after the three-day incident, it really was no bother.

I got him down and then lay him across my lap for a long, long time. And I held him in my arms. Just quietly held him in my arms and sometimes mibby brushed a strand of hair away from his brow or gently caressed his arm or shoulder. It's a shame, because I was telling him the story about the huts, but he didn't get to hear it.

In one sense I was waiting for a seizure to come upon me, for me to forget moments or minutes or hours suddenly. But that didn't happen. I just held him gently and let him rest in my arms, like the Sam Taylor-Woods (now Taylor-Johnson) and Robert Downey Jr. *Pietà*, which I had seen the year before at the Hayward. Because I know that's what we looked like – not Taylor-Johnson and Downey Jr., I mean a *pietà* – but I wasn't doing it for art or to be able to tell the story as a *pietà*. I just knew that, by that stage, pity is all there is for this sad way for everything to have ended. Sadness and pity and holding him gently in my arms. That's all there is to do. There isn't anything more, anything else.

I was thinking about a time me and Douglas had been discussing Francis Bacon's frightening and animalistic *Fragment of a Crucifixion*. I had asked him why he hated Bacon's work in general and this one in particular so much.

'Because in Bacon,' he said, 'there's no hope of redemption.'

'Yes. And that amount of honesty is difficult to look at head on,' I said.

'Exactly,' he said.

I held him till my arms grew sore and I shifted his weight just to get some relief. I held him beyond the ache. I held him. And shifted his weight once more. And held him.

I held him.

I held him in my arms until it really was over.

I have to confess, for a long, long time afterwards, even during the trial and all that palaver, I didn't really want to say much about Douglas and what had happened between us. I was burying thoughts and sensations and generally suppressing memories. I think I had to. No one said anything to me that I shouldn't be. Sometimes it's so difficult to know what to do for the best, isn't it? If only there was some good information somewhere that told you how to act in this or that situation. I mean, there probably is some good information somewhere that says don't go crucifying people, no matter how good a piece of art you get out of it. I get it, but if only there was this information, this good book or something that laid it all out. Because I can tell you this, the Holy Bible, that's not the book. Not for me, anyway.

The solicitor tried to get me to speak in my own defence at the trial, and I gave it a go, honestly. Just not a very good go. I mean, I suspect you know better than me how utterly cracked you sound when you try to explain that two people were completely committed to an artistic endeavour and would give so much, everything, their lives, to that. And who can you refer to when trying to explain it, this total commitment? Vincent van Gogh? That just makes you sound even more cracked. And comparing yourself to Vincent, well, that's another story all by itself. I went quiet and stayed quiet. What's the point of bearing witness when it just buries you?

I let other people do the talking. All the debates. Should we let her do this, should we let her do that? Should she be getting this or that or the next thing? Everything. I let others do the talking about everything. Well, everything except about my boy. But I won't... I mean, I can't... I won't talk about that just now. I mean, God, yes, I had done a wrong thing, but what a piece of art had been achieved! I tell you, if you want to see what a man being crucified is like, go out and crucify one. You'll see soon enough. And the painting I got out of it. Holy Jesus! You have no idea!

So mibby you're thinking about why I'm going through it all now, for your benefit? Well, mibby just the passage of time. Mibby wanting, finally, to explain all of what I've been telling you and how it led to the art that it did. I mean, I know all that stuff about not explaining art, about how the first failure of art is to *not* name a piece *Untitled*, because to need to title it means that the image or sculpture or installation or whatever it is cannot explain itself, cannot *be itself*. As someone once told me, it's like a kid making a line drawing and then writing underneath it 'A DOG'. If it was clear enough that the drawing was of a dog, why label it? And Douglas used to say, even numbers, and especially the Roman numerals I had taken to using for reasons I can't remember, *Untitled I*, *Untitled II… Untitled XV*, that was all just crap too. He said, 'Just go for *innumeri*, which means unnumbered,' which isn't exactly the right translation from the Latin, but, hey, whatever.

And not that I'm that sure that anything I've told you over the last wee while could really explain *The Mythopoeia of Christ*. But the problem word there is 'explain', isn't it? If I could, mibby I'd just show you the painting and then you'd have all the explanation you need. You'd see it in the expression on Douglas's face, on the spasm in his muscles, the twisted rictus girn, the pain, the suffering. The look on his face that says he doesn't want to be there, wants to be anywhere else, even being in hell would be preferable, but he knows that this cannot be. I give Douglas credit for that look on his face, though he wasn't pretending. I made him feel that. But I also painted something, something about the realisation I had had that humiliating him was over and exalting him was what I now had to do. They're the two great traditions in Crucifixion paintings: humiliation and exaltation. The whole story I've just gone over with you had finally, finally taught me Douglas's beauty, his strength, his wisdom had to shine out from the humiliation I had wrought upon him. But is it explanation *enough*? You'd have your explanation in seeing whether I'd done the painting justice or not. You would stand in judgement of my painting and say whether I'd done it right or not, whether it was a good painting or not.

Truth is, it's just been easier to bury memories of him and what we did till now, and now it's easier to try to say out loud what went on. Easier on me, that is. I accept all the psychological stuff that Dr Aziz has been gently leading me to accept, believe me. But it had to be now, now that I've served most of my time. Because it had to and has to make no difference at all, no difference *at all*.

I bet you're wondering what my mithair made of all this, and mibby Douglas's mother as well. So do I. Neither of them have said much about it. Not to me, anyway. Mibby my mithair despairs to my faither and my brothers and sisters, and mibby Douglas's mother confides her thoughts to her children. Mibby.

What my mithair has said is, 'Confession is good for the soul, Susan Alison.' You'd think that would be from the Bible, wouldn't you? But, like loads of things she says, like 'Hate the sin and not the sinner', 'The Lord helps those who help themselves', 'God moves in mysterious ways', 'As you make your bed, so must you lie in it', 'There is none so blind as she who will not see', 'Neither a borrower nor a lender be' and 'Hell hath no fury like a woman scorned', it's not from the Bible. 'Open confession is good for the soul' is actually an old Scots proverb. Oh, is it, now, confession? Is it good for the soul? As Douglas used to say when you told him that this or that thing was great or good or rubbish or bad, 'I'll be the judge of that.' And, I'm sorry, but I'll be the judge of me, if you don't mind. I know the story the way only me and Douglas could know it. I've told you it now, sure, but, like I said, you should crucify someone if you *really* want to know what that looks and sounds and smells and feels like – there's no way I could tell you what it felt like. I could try. Douglas could have told you as well, I suppose. We lived through it. But I'm not telling. The best I can tell you is, if you want an inkling what it might *look* like, go see my painting. It's touring at the moment. But, other than that, you'll need to find out for yourself.

Anyway, I've said what I've said because it makes no difference at all. And it's why I've been telling you.

INNUMERI

Well, there you go. That's about it for this story, which, if I had painted the scenes instead of telling you about it, I'd have called them a series of untitleds, *Untitled I*, *Untitled II*... I'm sure you can figure out the progression from there, because it all speaks for itself, really, doesn't it? And I've tried not to skip any of the details, like the way my mithair likes a story to be told. Any of the best details, anyway. And I've tried not to add a wee bit here and a wee bit there and other thoughts and ideas that overlay or underlie this theme or that. And I'll keep trying to do that, even though it means that sometimes I've left things a bit sketchy and with flaws here and there, but I know I'll mess it up if I go on. Like I thought there would be more about sectarianism here, but *I* don't have anything to say about that, it turns out. And I thought there would be more about Stephen and mibby even more about Patrick and possibly about his – Patrick's – strange friend Simon, who's not in this story at all, and about... well, about a lot of things, really. I thought I was going to tell you about Patrick's musician friends, the ones who almost made it, got signed by Creation, but by their mid-twenties were back working in the record shop Fopp

195

and bitter as hell about the music business, but only because it was such a sad story. It doesn't have any thematic resonance with the rest of the stuff I'm telling you. At least, I don't *think* so. And I remember now, I wanted to hit you with Stephen's brilliant comment when I was complaining about Douglas, the inorganic chemistry expert, the child prodigy sketcher, and prodigious portrait painter, the rich and successful conceptual artist, the generous humanitarian and thoughtful and practical political activist (he'd by the time left the Socialist Workers to join the Labour party, and was sending hundreds of thousands of pounds back from New York for various causes, which I knew and Stephen knew, though all the money was sent without the public knowing) and I had said to Stephen, 'What can't the guy do? What's he *bad* at?' And Stephen was like, 'Have you ever seen him dancing?' But that's me starting again, isn't it? Adding wee bits? I'm going to ruin it. I'll shut up soon.

And, anyway, you probably know the bits that come after this, from newspapers and magazines and television reports and profiles and stuff like that, like the Lynne Ramsey film based on our story *with a Mogwai soundtrack*, by the way! Oh my God. It was beautiful and poetic. Mibby you know the film or mibby just the music. OK, so it was shot from Douglas's POV, but that was to be suspected. Lynne and him were friends back in the day, you know? He still harboured dreams back then of becoming a video artist like Bill Viola, sculpting in time, as Tarkovsky has it.

No one knows how salvation will come, do they? But we can save the nostalgia for later.

You probably know that I won the Turner Prize too. A couple of years back, in 2020. Of course, the work I won for had to be about repentance, but that was inevitable, wasn't it, since I had to accept it from behind bars? I don't think they could have given it to me if the work hadn't been about repentance. And you probably know that, apart from the way other things are for me now, I'm a respected artist, renowned for my special kind of savage commitment. That's the part they always put in, 'savage commitment', just like they always say that Douglas MacDougal's work is known for the 'elemental' quality. 'Elemental.' Always that. What did that mean, anyway?

My 'savage commitment' was, of course, based in no small part on *The Mythopoeia of Christ*, my painting of the Crucifixion with Douglas as Jesus. I think really what they mean is the savagery of the suffering depicted, the suffering Christ. And because people started knowing that I had actually crucified Douglas to achieve the effects of the painting, well… It just came on like *whoosh*: fame, approbation, critical plaudits, scathing criticism, denunciation, death threats. You name it. My prices went through the roof. And I didn't just win the Turner Prize. There was the 2003 Venice Biennale, the solo shows in galleries in New York and Berlin and Melbourne and Paris and all that came after that. And always at the centre was *The Mythopoeia*. Always Douglas, right there, at the centre of it all, and where he always will be, living on through the years and decades and centuries, in art, my crucified Jesus.

And at the same time, I'm sure you heard about and mibby even followed the trial, the arrest and conviction, the plea for the needs of art and what the hell was I thinking and what was Douglas thinking, and Douglas's whole family dressed head to toe in black every day in the public gallery. And Lord Justice General Rodger's summation and the guilty verdict. You've probably heard about my time in Cornton Vale and now in Polmont, and how my conviction called for a life sentence, because of both my wilful and reckless regard for human life, and something about the cruel and unusual circumstances of the case. Basically, apart from anything else, they were saying I had tortured Douglas. I thought that 'cruel and unusual' was just some United States constitution thing, but, no, the Lord Justice General assured me that in Scotland it went right back to the final treatment and punishment of William Wallace. So, big stuff, you know? And then the outcry and the backlash and the jeering crowds and the sensationalist journalism that meant a hop, skip and a jump from the headline 'Bizarre art act' to 'Bizarre failed art suicide pact goes wrong'. And the forced *vox populi* that threw up probably the most outlandish of the outlandish theories, the claim by one church minister that I was evidence of the re-emergence of witchcraft in Scotland. Nut. A heid full of broken bottles and wee lassies' knickers. It was a total letters to the *Metro* deal. You probably know, too, that the prison authorities, after a lot of back and forth and this and that, let me paint still. Though I'm not allowed to earn a penny from *The Mythopoeia of Christ*, because there are laws out there to prohibit offenders benefiting from their crime. And I think, all things considered, I'll be out of here in a few years, mibby even next year. My solicitor stays hopeful.

Anyway, even with the original handing-down, when Lord Justice General Rodger said he must consider a sentence of 'life', I wasn't thinking of my life or even Douglas's life. I was thinking of two of Douglas's pieces,

1991's *HUMANS I* and 1999's *BODY BAGS*. *HUMANS I* was the first of a series of pieces where he filled bags with urine to the weight of an adult person, and then filled gallery spaces with these bags, lying around the floor, stacked up against the walls, suspended from the ceiling. To begin with this would be forty bags, say. By the end of the series, in 1999, there were hundreds at a time, piled high in gallery spaces. *BODY BAGS* was an update of a smaller work he had completed in 1992, *BODY BAG*, which had a single military body bag suspended in an otherwise empty gallery space and which was a comment on the war in Bosnia. *BODY BAGS* was a comment on the Kosovo crisis and this time a hundred or more military body bags hung from the ceiling in a darkened room. And I was thinking, for the first time, really, how eerie that exhibition had been, the darkness, the silence, the bags of urine the weight of a human adult. And for the first time, thinking of this, thinking about how his work was about *life*, as I was being sentenced for having crucified Douglas, I felt overwhelmed with love for him and his art, and moved by his art, falling in love with him and the work for the first time. And I was almost laughing, thinking it couldn't all have been his own urine by this stage, he had to be using other people's. And if that was the case, was it really his art any more? I looked over at the public gallery.

Lord Justice General Rodger was addressing me directly. 'Your tears now are too little, too late, I'm afraid.' And I was about to correct him, explain my tears, explain the deep ocean of love that I felt for Douglas and for his art. But I thought, what does it matter – what does anything matter except the art? And I said, 'Yes. I mean, no, Your Honour.'

And he corrected me, saying, 'You don't address me as "Your Honour", young lady, you address me as "My Lord".' He was sort of benignly smiling at me, almost beatifically. I decided it was best to say nothing in response.

Because what matters is that the art goes on, isn't it? The work of the artist, the seeing of the world anew, because the most difficult thing to see is what's right there, in front of you, what's actually there. And to see more of what's in front of you. And more and more again, like Hockney says. We die, but the art goes on and we are resurrected in the art. All this art that outlives the artists and the models by hundreds, thousands, mibby tens of thousands or even hundreds of thousands of years. If it were me continuing Douglas's project today, I'd pile thousands of bags the weight of adults and children and babies, my estimated number of 152,000 body bags piled up in temples and synagogues and churches and mosques and other places of worship to signify the people killed because of their religious beliefs by people with different religious beliefs to them today, yesterday, tomorrow, next week. Because I see now that what Douglas's art and my art are about is the same as the meaning of the Crucifixion. I now understand this true meaning of Christ on the cross. We all die, but the stories we tell in art, like the story of Christ's Passion, survive down through the decades and centuries and millennia to tell us, this's who we are. Art is the miracle that the story survives, in good paintings and films and music, and in good sculptures and installations and all the imagined worlds in art, and, of course, in good books, like this.

Religious suffering is, at one and the same time, the expression of real suffering and a protest against real suffering. Religion is the sigh of the oppressed creature, the heart of a heartless world, and the soul of soulless conditions. It is the opium of the people.

The abolition of religion as the illusory happiness of the people is the demand for their real happiness. To call on them to give up their illusions about their condition is to call on them to give up a condition that requires illusions. The criticism of religion is, there- fore, in embryo, the criticism of that vale of tears of which religion is the halo.

(Quoted in *Artists in Revolt*)